I Am a Rotarian

Kihyon (Kim) Kim
김기현

To AG Katie,
Light up Rotary!
Kim Kim

Printed in the United States of America

First Edition

ISBN-13: 978-0692218013 (Custom)
ISBN-10: 0692218017

ALSO BY KIHYON (KIM) KIM

My Life in Letters: The Extraordinary Journey of an Ordinary Man from Korea

Books published by Kim Kim are available at quantity discounts for educational, fund-raising, and special sales use. Please email: rotariankim@yahoo.com or write: Kim Kim, 146 Chipwood Dr. Hendersonville, TN 37075. USA.

Dedication

I dedicate this book to the memory of my two fathers. My biological father, Jae Young Kim, had never been a member of Rotary Club, but he lived as if he was born to be a Rotarian. He was a servant, and "Service Above Self" was his way of life. "Dad, I miss you and think about you every waking moment."

S.T. Womeldorf was a Rotarian who invited me to the Hendersonville Rotary Club and groomed me to be a leader. I followed him every step in Rotary and held the same positions he held in Rotary except one, being a District Governor. He told me I would be his District Governor within five years. This is the fifth year, and I will become a District Governor. My two fathers are not here to celebrate with me, but I think I have made them proud.

Also, I would like to dedicate this book to my biological mother Jung Sook Kim and Rotary mother Mary Ann Womeldorf. Someone once said, "God could not be everywhere, so He created mothers." When I think of God, I think of my two mothers. I love you and thank you for being my mothers.

Introduction

If someone had told me that my letters were going to be written in English, rather than my native tongue, Korean, would ever be published in a book, I would not have even attempted to write the first letter. I would have felt defeated already, for I would have been overwhelmed by the many excuses such as: language barrier, lack of time, or the fact that no person will appreciate what I'm trying to do. I would have stared at blank sheet of paper hoping that magically, mystically, and effortlessly the words would pop out and express my heart.

It's true that I do not speak fluent English. So, how can I write in such a way that words come to me naturally? I do not even have time to write a letter every month to club members. As a club president, I choose to do something that not everyone is excited about; I set my personal goal of 100% Paul Harris Fellow Club for our goal for 2008-2009 to celebrate the 40th Anniversary of the Rotary Club of Hendersonville. I know not every member will donate a thousand dollars to eradicate polio. To ease the pain and to avoid discouragement, I started writing monthly letters to four of my non-critical and devoted supporters: my three young children and my wife. I mailed these letters to the homes of all the club members.

It is irrelevant now whether you are on board or not after reading the various letters in this book. This is my personal goal and it means a lot to me. Abraham Lincoln said, "The probability that we may fail in the struggle ought not to deter us from the support of a cause we believe to be just." My only wish is for all members of all the Rotary clubs in every city in America to march with me to eradicate polio. I dedicate this book to you for the accomplishment of being a Paul Harris

Fellow and to celebrate the 40th Year Anniversary of the Rotary Club of Hendersonville, Tennessee, U.S.A.

I want to say thank you to my three children for being Paul Harris Fellows and my wife for being a Major Donor. I love you so much! At last, I hope you enjoy reading and are touched by the stories in this book just as much as I enjoyed writing them. I am privileged to include some of Rotarians' personal stories in this book. Every story I read, I am touched and grateful to know such fine Rotarians in my life. While I was writing, I had a chance to revisit my past and to examine what I am doing today. I was a sculptor who created the most beautiful woman and fell in love with her. I cried over my own letters, not because they were well written, but because I lived my life whether it was good or bad. I do not know what is going to happen tomorrow, but one thing is absolute: I will live my God given life until He calls me Home.

I would love to hear from you and share my Rotary life with your club members. It will be my pleasure if you invite me to speak to your clubs and let me know how these stories affected you and share your stories with me. You can send your stories; rotariankim@yahoo.com.

Kim Kim
146 Chipwood Dr,
Hendersonville, TN 37075
USA

TABLE OF CONTENTS

PART ONE: LETTERS TO ROTARIANS

PART TWO: LETTERS TO PRESIDENTS-ELECT

PART THREE: LETTERS FROM ROTARIANS

PART ONE

LETTERS TO ROTARIANS

40TH Year Anniversary

On June 16, 1969, the Rotary Club of Hendersonville was chartered. District Governor George Dehoff (1971-1972) wrote: "Hendersonville: A young, growing club on the way up in Rotary." Forty years later, the "young and growing club" of two dozen men has grown to nearly 170 men and women from every walk of life who share a common desire to make a difference.

In this book, you will see how Rotarians have put the motto *Service Above Self* into action. You will see how Rotarians are dedicated to improving the quality of life for everyone in our community, especially those whose needs are often overlooked. You will learn about the causes we support and the fundraisers we sponsor. You will learn about the organizations that benefit from our support such as the Hendersonville Library, Community Child Care, Samaritan Center, college scholarships, Books from Birth, Salvus Center, Relay for Life, Christmas for Kids, Wheels in Motion, Dictionary Project for every 3rd grader in Sumner County, and more.

You will see that the Hendersonville Rotary's humanitarian reach does not stop at the Sumner County line. The club is actively involved in projects that make life better for people all over the world. More than thirty people travel to Guatemala each year for a dental, medical, and vision mission that the Hendersonville Rotary Club started sixteen years ago. You will learn about Rotary International, which sponsors relief projects on a global scale.

The Shelterbox Response Team (SRT) is a Rotary International project that provides humanitarian aid in the form of shelter, warmth, comfort, and dignity to people displaced by natural and manmade disasters. Through my involvement, I have had the opportunity to see firsthand how the network of 1.2 million Rotarians in over 33,000 clubs in 200 countries makes it possible to build goodwill and peace in the world.

I have never met Rotarian Robert Ellis, but every time I drive by Ellis Middle School, it reminds me the of Rotary club's past. When current Rotary International President Dong Kurn Lee attended our club meeting in April, 2009, and visited the Rotary Fountain in Memorial Park as a tribute to fallen officers, it reminded me of today's Rotary. As for tomorrow, we Rotarians are sowing seeds for the future. Though we may not be around to enjoy the fruit of the trees we plant today our children will, and that is enough for me.

It has been an honor and a privilege to lead the Hendersonville Rotary Club during this pivotal year. The future of both community and Rotary are in our hands. Join us to celebrate the next 40 years of *Service Above Self.*

First Letter

One of the responsibilities assigned to the president of the Rotary Club of Hendersonville is being in charge of supporting the Rotary Foundation through participation, financial contribution, and developing club leaders capable of serving in Rotary.

A Rotarian said, "The more I learn about Rotary, the more I love Rotary." To me, the more I learn, the more I realize that I am only scratching the surface of the ocean called Rotary. It's a long journey to accomplish our Rotary mission, but it is worth taking small steps toward a long journey because every story that you and I have is worth sharing with other people. Mother Teresa once said, "The whole work is only a drop in the ocean. But if I did not put the drop back in, the ocean would be one drop less."

I believe we each have to row our own boat to reach our destination called the ocean. If I stop rowing my boat in the middle of the journey because of the fear of failure and obstacles, the ocean will be one boat less in the end. The boat in the harbor may be safe and secure, but it wasn't built for that reason. It has to leave the safe harbor and face all the obstacles even if all our Rotary work is only a drop in the ocean.

As you know, I have a great passion for Paul Harris Fellow (PHF). After I became a Paul Harris Fellow, it literally changed my life and my attitude toward Rotary. After I realized I was a part of eradicating polio, a part of humanitarian service in Guatemala, and a part of rescuing children from poverty and illiteracy, I no longer considered myself as a member of the

Rotary club but a Rotarian for life. Most of all, I was a part of the Rotary family. As you can see, I was happy for being a Paul Harris Fellow, and it was selfish of me to keep all the happiness and self-actualization to myself. The best way to multiply happiness is to divide it and share it with fellow Rotarians so that we can experience the greatest joy of giving and sharing together. I designated all my contributions to the Polio Plus program because my cousin in Korea was paralyzed when he was only three years old-polio crippled his life.

Thanks to financial contribution, ninety-nine percent of the world is polio-free. As of 2007, only four countries-Afghanistan, India, Nigeria, and Pakistan are endemic for the poliovirus. We have to fight for children and give to the Rotary Foundation because no child is safe from this deadly disease as long as one case of polio remains in the world. Your one thousand dollar contribution buys the polio vaccine for two thousand babies in those countries.

As of November 2007, there are forty-seven Paul Harris Fellows and twenty-three sustaining members in our club. Fifty-six non-Rotarians became Paul Harris Fellows and fifty-nine non-Rotarians are sustaining members; non-Rotarians contributed more than active Rotarians. Next Rotary year of 2008-2009, our club is celebrating our 40th year anniversary. What a great legacy it will be to have 100 % Paul Harris Fellow Club.

The best time to plant an oak tree is twenty years ago. The next best time is now. I'd like to share a story with you. A missionary came to a little village in Korea after traveling through many other countries. She came upon the most beautiful tree she had ever seen, and then she stopped a young man passing by and asked for the name of a tree. The young man said it was Gomoknamu. She asked him if he could help her plant the tree in her back yard so that she could enjoy watching it everyday. The young man burst out laughing and said, "That is crazy. It takes one hundred years for that tree to be matured." She thought for a moment and said to him, "In that case, I want to plant it right now."

You and I are enjoying this beautiful tree called Rotary because somebody planted it one hundred years ago for us. We will never get to see the tree we planted, but our children and the next generations will. An unknown author said, "If I live and do the things for myself, everything dies with me. If I live and do the things for others and the world, everything remains and never dies. It stays with them-in their heart."

My fellow Rotarians, my belief in you and my dream of 100 % Paul Harris Fellow Club might not come true if we think we can't. However, I say to you that false belief is better than disbelief. False dreams are better than not dreaming because tomorrow will come to those who believe and dream that it can be done. Thank you for being a Paul Harris Fellow. If you are not, please become one, and together we can celebrate our 40th year anniversary on June 16, 2009. That will be the one of greatest legacies.

If Not Now, Then When?

Last year I enjoyed reciting "The Thought of the Day" at the end of our weekly Rotary meetings. I vividly remember the quote by Sarak Kirby Trimmer, "Every living creature that comes into the world has something allotted him to perform, therefore he should not stand an idle spectator of what others are doing."

I truly believe every human being is born with a reason and purpose in life. Why I was born and the meaning of my life can only be found and answered by myself. I have felt that I have wasted my life searching for the answer, but now, because of Rotary, I have found the reason and purpose of my life in this world.

It really does not matter how small my life is compared to someone else who contributed and influenced a great deal in this world. It is my life. My life, as a Rotarian, is worth living and should be shared with a fellow Rotarian like you, who not only understands life but also enriches every person you touch.

You should know by now of my passion for Paul Harris Fellow (PHF). In 2007, President Eddie, Foundation Chair Art, Secretary Robin, and many Paul Harris Fellows were working very hard to reach our goal; 100% PHF Club to celebrate our 40th year anniversary in June 16, 2009.

What does my being a Paul Harris Fellow have to do with you? Do you wonder why it is so important to me for you to become Paul Harris Fellows? Six months after I joined Rotary Club in 2000, my business went bankrupted. I was forced to close down my business and lost everything I had, including my home. In the following week I came to a Rotary meeting to say good bye since I no longer was able to pay the membership dues and was not able to face members who had supported and believed in me.

The Foundation Chair in our club, Bill Sinks, put his arm around me and said, "Would you like to be a member of Paul Harris Fellow by contributing one thousand dollars to the Rotary Foundation?" I was so mad at him and thought he had to be crazy to ask me such a thing at the worst time of my life. How could he ask me to contribute one thousand dollars when I could not even provide food on the table for my family? I had no home or a job, but I still had hopes and dreams. I realized there were many things that I was thankful for even if I lost everything. As long as I had hopes and dreams, nobody could take that away from me.

Then I began to think, " IF NOT NOW, THEN WHEN?" That was the lowest point of my life, and I wanted to do something for others. I decided to become a Paul Harris Fellow. I do not know how I came up with one-hundred dollars a week, but I did. Within six months, I became a Paul Harris Fellow. It is a wonderful reward to see the fruit of my contribution touch other people and become a seed to the humanitarian action. Our contribution to Paul Harris Fellows made it possible for Doran Lee, the recipient of the Cultural Ambassadorial Scholarship (her story is mentioned in later letters) to come to the United States to study first hand and learn about American culture.

Fellow Rotarians, will you be the one who contributes to our goal by reaching 100% Paul Harris Fellow Club? Or will you be "an idle spectator of what others are doing"? We have forty seven Paul Harris Fellows in our club, and fifty six non Rotarians Paul Harris Fellows. When you are asked like Bill

Sinks asked me, "Would you like to be a member of Paul Harris Fellow by contributing one thousand dollars to the Rotary Foundation?" What is your answer going to be?

A Crippled Freshman

A freshman transferred to Kang Suh Middle School in the midst of a cold winter. One night I found him at the public bus stop. I was surprised to see him so late at night, knowing freshmen classes were over several hours before. However, I wasn't surprised to see him crippled with shining silver crutches.

This freshman reminded me of my cousin who was only three years old when polio crippled his entire life. Because my cousin was abandoned by his family, my parents took him in and educated him in a vocational school so that he could eventually support himself. I was familiar with his situation and the obstacles he faced; the freshman could not get on the bus by himself with a heavy school bag in his hand at the peak of rush hour. Furthermore, the bus drivers would not let him get on the bus because either there were no empty seats or they just did not want to wait a few extra minutes for a crippled man to get on board. That was how I met Sung Ha Kim. It became my voluntary duty to carry his school bag or even carry him on my back onto the bus whether in rain or snow.

Being a senior in middle school, I had to take extra curriculums and study long hours in preparation for a highly competitive, nation-wide high school entrance exam. My exam scores were compared to the entire middle school seniors' scores in Korea, and they determined which school I was qualified to enter. Failing the entrance exam not only brings disgrace onto the whole family but also prevents the pathway to success from the early stages of life.

As time went on, I started dreading going to school because I did not want to waste my valuable studying time at the bus stop to help Sung Ha Kim. I even intentionally missed classes sometimes or sneaked out of the rooms before the freshmen were let out Once I arrived at home I could not help but worry about him and wonder if he was still there at the bus stop waiting for me. I regretted what I had done with a heavy heart. "Why do I have to help him? He isn't my cousin. If he needs help getting home, his family should find someone else," I justified my action.

When my parents asked why I was getting home late, I finally told my dad that I wanted to help the freshman but not every day because it interfered with my school work and my personal life. After listening to my complaints, my dad said, "When Mom and I took your cousin in, it was very difficult for us to accept him." He had complained about having to take care of his nephew all his life and even confronted God that he wasn't his father. One day he realized God might have looked down on earth and searched for the best parents for this child. My dad believed that God thought he was the best father for his nephew. Although my cousin's body was crippled and needed endless attention and care, he was a beautiful child and perfect in every way. Listening to my dad, I realized I should have been thankful for the opportunity to help him, and I accepted that I might just as well have been chosen to be the best caretaker for him as long as he needed me.

I was eagerly looking forward to my graduation before I knew him, but it came too soon and I had to say good bye. Sung Ha Kim came to my ceremony with his mother, and I soon found out that his younger sister had polio too; thus, his mother had to take care of her as well.

His mother cried and thanked my parents for what I did for her son for the last five months, rain or snow. Of course, my sisters were in shock to hear that their selfish, no-good brother actually helped another person. All my friends were cheering and celebrating for the end of the school year. I thought I should have been too, for I was being freed from a heavy burden and a moral responsibility. I was suddenly filled with so much emotion, and I dreaded the end. I wanted to apologize to his mother and my parents because there were so many days that I selfishlessly ran away from him and refused to help. I was angry at myself for realizing too late, and I was sad that I was no longer able to help him. I felt I was taken away the most precious gift.

Rotarians all over the world have contributed more than $630 million to the Polio Plus program since 1985. One thousand children were infected by the disease daily, but now 99 % of the world is polio free. If we fail to eradicate the remaining 1 %, 10 million children will be paralyzed over the next 40 years. There is no doubt in every Rotarian's mind that polio will have been eradicated from the face of the earth within a few years. Once that happens, people from all over the world will celebrate one of the biggest accomplishments in mankind, and 1.2 million Rotarians will be so proud of what each of us did to make a difference.

It has been said, "All of us are born for a reason, but all of us do not discover why. Success in life has nothing to do with what you gain in life or accomplish for yourself. It's what you do for others." The time to become a Paul Harris Fellow by donating a thousand dollars is right now. Every time I see someone crippled by polio, I remember Sung Ha Kim. He may not remember me after thirty years. He may not know that I still live with regret because I ran away and refused to help him when he needed me. For the rest of my life, I want to fill Sung Ha's lost days with hope, so I dream that one day no child will be affected by polio. Will you help? Will you do your part, my fellow Rotarians?

Arranged Marriage

When I was five years old, I moved to the small Korean village of Sang Do Dong. Between the sharp peaks and pointed paths of the mountains, there was a Buddhist monastery called Mi Ryuk Ahm, and that was my home. It was odd to have a house in the middle of the monastery and even stranger to have a small village boy living in the compound's isolation. Only Buddhist monks were permitted to live simple lives dedicated to spirituality. As the monks learned sutra and practiced a koan— a paradox or riddle used in Zen Buddhism that aims to break down logical reasoning. It is regarded as a road to enlightenment. I would play, scream, and yell the youthful exuberance of childhood in the silent but alive temple. The monks became my friends, teachers, and mentors. Naturally, I grew to love their lifestyle and dreamed of one day joining them. The monastery's master, Dae Sa Nim, took me under his wing, counseled me and groomed me for the sparse life of a Buddhist monk.

Although I lived in a Buddhist monastery, I attended a Christian school. By the age of 17, I had left Korea for an education in the United States. Ironically, I practiced Zen meditation while studying the Bible, and I believed in salvation only through Jesus Christ, even though I was studying reincarnation. Because Buddhism has been embedded in Korean culture and its people for thousands of years, it became inseparable to me. I truly believe Buddhist blood flowed through me, and I was predestined to become a monk. The picture of Jesus Christ was hung in my room and I clung harder to the Buddhism not to lose my identity.

While attending college in America, I still had dreamt of becoming a monk. As the oldest son, my family obligations and duties conflicted with my dreams of monastic life. My father's best friend, who had known me since birth, often joked that he would find me a wife one day. Korean culture often dictates arranged marriage and being the first born son of the Kim family, I knew I had to take care of my family and that I would marry a Korean woman. The family friend called from Korea with news that he had found my future bride, Myung Sook Lim. I was skeptical but could not disobey my parents' wish. I wrote to tell her she would be better off with someone more worthy. I wrote letters to her every week for a year. We were both very truthful with each other in our letters. I thought that if I was completely honest with her, she would surely turn me down. I had neither goodness about me nor accumulated wealth to get married, or so I thought. Instead, my letters only convinced Myung Sook that I was the one for her, and I eventually began to feel the same way toward her.

I proposed to her through a fifty page letter and returned to Korea to marry a woman I had never met. I was in college at that time, so it was difficult to convince my professors that I needed to go to Korea for a month to get married. I arrived at the airport and wondering who and where she was. When she approached me, she was more beautiful than I had ever imagined. We spent one month together until I had to come back to the United States alone. I obtained my citizenship and brought my wife to America a year later. I once dreamed of a life filled with solitude as a Buddhist monk, but now with my wife and three teenage children, I have enjoyed a life filled with love.

I have often been asked, "How can you love and marry someone whom you have never met?" I truly believe the one you marry is already determined by who you are. I did not get to choose my parents or my siblings. They were there to love me unconditionally and to be loved whole-heartedly in return. The other day, my wife asked out of curiosity what I would have done if she had been crippled, blind, or ugly when I saw her for the first time. I know from the bottom of my heart she married me for who I am. Even if she were handicapped, I would still have married her, loved her, cared for her, and shared my life with her.

Sharing this personal story is for all of us to recognize our combined human, cultural, and generational diversity; we need to embrace the differences among us. Desiderata said, "You are a child of the universe, no less than the trees and the stars, you have a right to be here." Because we are unique human beings, each of us is worth telling his own story. We have a different belief system and were raised in different cultures. That makes us who we are.

Culture is defined as the set of values, beliefs, and customs that people have in common with other members of society. It is the primary means by which humans adapt to their environments. According to that definition, people in that society share and maintain their unique culture by learned behaviors. America is made of many subcultures that are significantly different from dominant cultures within the same society. At first, newcomers to America are forced to lose their cultural differences in order to "melt" into an existing American culture. Some voluntarily abandon their cultural traditions to become new Americans.

Society cannot exclude certain cultures because of their differences and our ignorance. The American society cannot be maintained by melting together or assimilating people into one. Individual's unique and separate identity should be accepted and maintained by the society no matter where he comes from. In order to enrich our own lives and to accept other people's ways of life, we must understand different cultures and actively participate in organizations that promote and embrace different cultures. That is why Rotary Clubs in over 200 countries play a vital part. There are 1.2 million Rotarians and over 33,000 Rotary clubs. No matter where we are in the world, we are welcome into the fellowship and accepted as who we are.

The world historian, Will Durant, said, "The time when you need to do something is when no one else is willing to do it, when people are saying it can't be done." You had already shown it could be done when you invited me to our Rotary club when others turned me down. You proved it once again when you selected me as the first Korean American president. The Rotary way of life is "Service Above Self," and living by the Four-Way Test. Since the first time I was invited to be a member of the Rotary club in 2000, I have loved being a Rotarian and everything about it. I am so thankful for the opportunity to serve people and to help our community and communities in other countries. I plead with you for Paul Harris Fellow more than a year ago and announced my personal goal as president of our club in 2008-2009. Now it is the time to show and prove to the world that it can be done by accomplishing 100% Paul Harris Fellow Club.

I gave up my dreams of being a Buddhist monk. After I accepted Jesus Christ as my Savior, I was born again and I could not help but love all of my life and appreciate what Rotary has done for me. To me, being a Rotarian is being a true Christian because I get to fulfill God's work, Service Above Self. Mary Frances Berry said, "Some men have thousands of reasons why they cannot do what they want to, when all they need is one reason why they can". Do any of you still doubt why we need to become Paul Harris Fellows? Do you still think it cannot be done?

The Mission of the Rotary Foundation

What percentage of your membership dues do you think go to the Rotary Foundation? The answer is zero. Then, you obviously wonder how Rotary supports three main programs: Educational, Humanitarian Grants, and Polio Plus. Rotary International and the Rotary Foundation are two separate entities, and all three programs mentioned are supported by the Rotary Foundation. In other words, if we do not support the Rotary Foundation through both participation and financial contributions that make a difference in people's lives, the Rotary Foundation simply can not exist. Foundation programs are solely supported by voluntary contributions made by Rotarians and people around the world who share the vision and belief of Rotary.

I confess I have neither the knowledge nor experience to lead fellow Rotarians who are experienced and dedicated to the Rotary. My only hope is that my letters will be used as a necessary tool that can be helpful in educating, motivating, and inspiring other fellow Rotarians.

The mission of the Rotary Foundation is to support the efforts of Rotary International in the fulfillment of the object of Rotary, Rotary's mission, and the achievement of world understanding and peace through local, national, international humanitarian, educational, and cultural programs. Then what is Paul Harris Fellow? Paul Harris was the founder of the Rotary Club in Chicago in 1905. When he passed away in 1947, people from all over the world made contributions to honor the founder of Rotary. This ongoing desire to honor him led to the idea of Paul Harris Fellow Recognition in 1957. A Paul Harris Fellow is someone who contributes or in whose name is contributed 1,000 dollars. The distinctive Paul Harris Fellow medallion, lapel pins, and attractive certificate have become highly respected symbols of a substantial financial commitment to the Rotary Foundation by Rotarians and friends around the world.

World denoted and famous people such as Pope John Paul II, Mother Teresa, Nelson Mandela, Prince Charles of England, King Hussein of Jordan, and many more were named Paul Harris Fellows. More importantly, thousands of people like you and me whose names only few of us recognize choose to become Paul Harris Fellows out of their nameless acts of kindness and love. In 1968, the Trustees added a category called Sustaining Member for those who could not give the entire a thousand dollars, with pledge to giving additional contributions until a thousand dollars is reached. When sustaining members attain the $1,000, they become Paul Harris Fellow. By 1984, there were 100,000 Paul Harris Fellows. In 2006, the number of Paul Harris Fellows reached the one million mark.

Arch Klumph, father of the Rotary Foundation said, "We should look at the Foundation as being not something of today or tomorrow, but think of it in terms of the years and generations to come." To celebrate our club's 40 year anniversary on June 16, 2009, here are top ten ways to help you achieve Paul Harris Fellow membership.

1. Write a $1,000 check today to the Rotary Foundation.
2. Give a check of $20 a week to the Foundation chair in our club.
3. When you pay membership fees quarterly, pay an extra $250 to the Rotary Foundation.

4. Have the whole family collect spare change in a piggy bank.
5. Ask our treasurer to bill you $100 a month until $1,000 is reached.
6. On your anniversary, birthday, Valentine's Day, or Christmas, demand, "Show me the Paul Harris Fellow money."
7. No Starbucks coffee for six months.
8. If your company pays your Rotary membership dues, you pay the same amount to the Rotary Foundation.
9. Tell Kim Kim, "Me no speaking Englishee" pretending you do not understand what he is talking about.
10.   Ask Kim Kim to resign or kick him out of the Rotary club if you think 100% PHF can't be done. I will not rest until the goal is met.

If I Die Tomorrow (I)

My time of writing monthly letters to my fellow Rotarians has come to an end, but your time has just begun to take action. If you have not decided to become a Paul Harris Fellow, I can only blame myself and feel disappointed for my failure to convey the true meaning of Rotary and my passion for Paul Harris Fellow. I apologize to all present and past Paul Harris Fellows who believed I could change and inspire other Rotarians. I know I let them down by not reaching 100% Paul Harris Fellow Club yet.

John Stephen Akhwari was a marathon runner from Tanzania, representing his country in the 1968 Summer Olympics in Mexico City. Shortly after the race began, he fell and had serious injuries on both legs. The medical staff treated and bandaged his open wound and asked him to quit the race due to the seriousness of his injury. He refused to give up, got on the trail and ran with dragging feet. All of the other marathon runners had already finished several hours ago, and all the medals had been given out at the closing ceremony. Because they did not realize there was a last runner, there were hardly any spectators in the stadium by the time he arrived. He finally crossed the finish line and raised both arms in the air, walking the final victory lap.

A reporter saw both tears of pain and of victory in his face when he approached John to ask why he did not give up knowing he would be the last, and there was no chance of winning a medal. John answered, "My country did not send me five thousand miles to start the race. They sent me five thousand miles to finish the race." 75 runners started the race, winning a gold medal in their minds. John finished 57th. Whatever the reason, 18 of them dropped out the race. Forty-one years later today, people do not remember who won gold, silver, or bronze medal, but we remember John because he finished his race against all odds and inspired all of us. His name will never be forgotten. Our race to eradicate polio has begun more than twenty years ago, and we are getting so close to crossing the finish line. We cannot give up now and leave it to somebody else because no one but you can finish your own race. One lap to go! Let's finish what we started so we all can walk the victory lap together.

The following is an essay I wrote one winter in 1988 before I left for Korea to marry a woman I had never met. I wonder if I still have such an undying passion for life in me or if I have given up and sold my heart to the world. It would be much easier to express my feelings and thoughts in my native tongue. Speaking and writing in English is not as natural and free as Korean for me. I am not sure if I could convince all Koreans who read my letters to march the path to be Paul Harris Fellows either.

Abraham Maslow says, "A musician must make music, an artist must paint, a poet must write, if he is to be ultimately at peace with himself." Is it absurd to ask Rotarians to be Rotarians? Is it absurd to ask human beings to be human beings? It is our human nature that is embedded in our genes to help the dying and to give food to a hungry child.

If I Die Tomorrow (II)

Looking out the window, I see snow falling down to the ground, and children playing on the playground covered with white snow, throwing snowballs and chasing after one another. I turn my head to watch MTV. A song is playing even though there is no audience. All of my attention is outside, watching a bird building a nest on a white pine tree; it is the red breasted robin.

I know the story about the robin. A man loved a woman with all his heart but could not show his feelings toward her, for he was too timid. Most of all, he was afraid she might not love him as much as he loved her. He sat on a lonely hill every night and began writing a poem to a star. He wrote a poem which could not return to him. Finally, he believed that his love would never be accomplished as long as he lived, so he jumped down to the ground and killed himself. At that time, the goddess of love was watching and felt pity for him. She poured life-giving water on his body and said to him, "Be whatever you want to be." His hands and feet went red first and then his whole body turned scarlet. He climbed the lonely hill on which he wrote the poem and jumped up into the sky only to fly. That was how he became a red bird, the robin. I do not care what people say. I believe that to be true.

I carefully examined my hand. The reason why my hand was not red like a robin was probably because I did not love with all my heart. No, that can't be true. I must not change my heart while I love someone. After I die, I will be like the robin.

Death? What will I be after I die? Is there a life beyond death? If I die tomorrow, would today be the same? Could I still see snow and children making everything beautiful? Snow and children might still be here on earth, and a robin may continue brooding on eggs as well. But, in any case, I would not be with them. No one in the world is going to remember me. People do not even remember the name of a flower they loved once. I, however, will remember and miss everything that I am facing at this moment.

If I die tomorrow, what shall I do? I wonder what people would say about me. Would they say that I was kind and loved my wife and family? Would they say that I tried my best? What would I miss the most? I do not want to spend my last minutes creating something so that the rest of the world remembers me. I want to cry over my unfinished poem of life.

I would absolutely miss my wife and my family since they are part of my life. Also, I would miss a book *Little Prince* and his words, "What is essential is invisible to the eyes." Late at night I listen to the "1812 Overture" and "Madame Butterfly." Suddenly I am in the battlefield, hearing the cannonball fired in the year of 1812. Then, I burst into the house to save Madame Butterfly who is about to cut her throat. Oh! I am terrified as soon as I imagine I no longer hear this music. What about my unborn child? Could I still watch and talk to the rising sun? When the sun rises behind my back, I stop to confront him. "You give sunlight and lighten all nature, but why can't you lighten my life or burn me? The sun appears to be laughing at me; otherwise, he tries to comfort me. I think that he is beautiful anyway.

There are too many things for me to miss and to accomplish. My body might be dead and buried under the ground or spread onto the shore by the sea which I always loved to stroll, but my soul will never die unless I see that someone appreciated my poems in his heart and changed his life. That would be what I miss most when tomorrow comes.

I do not want to blame anybody or ask why I must die. I was the happiest child when I was born, but now I feel like abandoned. How foolish I was! I thought that I could live forever. When the one I loved passed away, others followed in her footsteps. It is my turn now, but until it's over, I will help the robin build a nest and read my poem to a man who wants to love, not to be loved. If I can do that, I will neither live in vain nor regret yesterday, today, or tomorrow. That is what I want from today.

I close my eyes for a minute and open slowly. I see snow, children, a robin, and me. They are different from what I saw yesterday. I will not worry about tomorrow and what is going to happen. I will live as best as I can today, and give you all I have. I will die peacefully and beautifully. I will be leaving you tomorrow, but you, will not let me go. I will always be in your heart.

"I do not ask for the meaning of the song of a bird or the rising of the sun on a misty morning. There they are, and they are beautiful."

Pete Hamill

If I can stop one heart from breaking,
I shall not live in vain;
If I can ease one life the aching,
Or cool one pain,
Or help one fainting robin
Unto his nest again,
I shall not live in vain.

By Emily Dickinson

내가 만일 한 마음의 상처를 멈추게 할 수 있다면
나의 삶은 헛되지 않을 것이다.
내가 만일 한 생명의 고통을 덜게 할 수 있다면
내가 한 사람의 고통을 식힐 수가 있다면
또는 내가 숨져 가는 한 마리 라빈을
그 보금자리에 다시 살게 한다면
나의 삶은 결코 헛되지 않을 것이다.

시인 에밀리 딕킨슨

After the Last Letter

Last November, I set out to write a monthly letter to all members until my time to preside the following year. I carried out my responsibility as a president-elect and gave full support to President Eddie Roberson and his goal; at the same time, I needed to prepare for my presidency and to work out the strategic plan for my goal.

In order to have a successful year, it is imperative for members to not only know the club goal for the upcoming year, while accomplishing the goal in hand, but also to get involved right away from the beginning as the new Rotary year starts. I, first and foremost, was interested in their passions and attitudes toward Rotary.

We are chosen to be Rotarians and to spread the ideal of service in our personal, business, and community life. We must have the highest ethical standard in everything we do. Thus, the role of president, I believe, is to help members be representatives of the Rotary organization. People will know Rotary by how we live by our core values, and the community will judge Rotary by our actions. What we do everyday should contribute to giving our life and people's lives something meaningful. If we do not, we are not true Rotarians. In order to meet my objective, I carefully considered what the most effective way to convince members was. I decided that was to send monthly letters to all members. I did not think it would deter or interfere this year's goal while I was working on mine.

The previous letter, *If I Die Tomorrow* was the last letter sent to all members. There was no need for me to continue monthly letters because of two reasons: first, my motive had changed from the original scheme, and second, I could easily and directly communicate with them anytime once I became president. That was July 2008, and I, somehow, have not stopped writing my letters, knowing I have no intention of sending them to members.

Why do I still stay up late at night and go through painful fights for words? I am beaten by a ghost and bleeding from a self-inflicted wound, searching for words that express my heart. At first, I focused on how I could change, encourage, and inspire members to be Paul Harris Fellows by sharing my personal stories and my beliefs. The circle of influence and social status of all members were too vastly important to be ignored. I began to believe in myself as one member after another was persuaded by my truthfulness in writing and passion for life.

I wondered whether I could turn them into be true Rotarians, who not only believe in Service Above Self but also live by Four-Way Test in all aspects of their lives. The Four-Way Test of the things we think, say or do: first, is it the truth? Second, is it fair to all concerned? Third, will it build good will and better friendships? Fourth, will it be beneficial to all concerned? People do not have to be members of Rotary Clubs to be Rotarians. In fact, there are members who join for the wrong reasons and do not believe in Rotary's motto: Service Above Self. Anyone who has a heart of Rotary's ideal of service and lives by Four-Way Test, is a true Rotarian. I could clearly see the enormous fruit of our efforts, improving the quality of life for others; thus, I sprang at members with ferocity, without being considerate of their feelings and their circumstances. I have fallen into self-absorption and been blinded by self-assurance.

Johann Wolfgang Von Goethe says, "I am, however, growing daily more aware how foolish it is to judge others by one's own standards. Ah, I am glad to let others go their ways. If only they would allow me to do the same." Looking back, I realize how foolish I was to believe I could change and motivate members one by one.

"Why do you look at the speck of sawdust in your brother's eye and pay no attention to the plank in your own eye? How can you say to your brother, 'Let me take the speck out of your eye,' when all the time there is a plank in your own eye? You hypocrite, first take the plank out of your own eye, and then you will see clearly to remove the speck from your brother's eye." (Matthew 7: 3-5)

To cleanse an impure heart, there must be a pure heart that can't be easily soiled. My heart is too soiled to cleanse other persons, and I lack many qualities in all aspects of my life to influence them.

To be honest, 100% Paul Harris Fellow Club is not what I was destined to achieve this year; I wanted each and every member to be a true Rotarian. While all of us are trying to be Paul Harris Fellows, I thought this unselfish act of Service Above Self-serving and putting others first- would make us rediscover our forgotten self, true Rotarians.

The ultimate goal is to find what we are and why we are doing what we do as Rotarians. We rarely find what we are searching for at the summit. It is found while we are climbing the mountain. Someone said, "I have learned that everyone wants to live on top of the mountain, but all the happiness and growth occurs while you are climbing it." Our goal and our success should never be a destination. It is our journey toward the summit in which we find ourselves and happiness. It does not matter how many times we have reached the summit. If we failed to recognize why we are doing it, we, standing at the summit, get to discover that our goal was no use, and we hadn't accomplished what we truly set out to do. It might take some members years to be Paul Harris Fellows by contributing one thousand dollars, but as long as we know the purpose of why we must do and work toward that goal one step at a time, the goal is already accomplished. If then, personal and club goals such as 100% Paul Harris Fellows, once believed to be impossible to achieve, become the smallest and easiest tasks to all Rotarians.

Members who realize our potential and our capability can accomplish anything and can change the world because the possibility is unlimited now since we endured hardship and experienced the true meaning of Rotary. We cannot change the world unless we change ourselves first. There is an old saying in Korea, Gha wha man sa sung. It means that if you are peaceful or harmonious, you can accomplish anything in the world.

I know I offend some members, and some might have left the club because of my failure to convey what I am trying to build within you. My poor leadership misguided you, and my written and verbal communication skills probably made it worse. If I am told over and over again by someone who does not live by what he preaches, that I have to live by certain ways and do certain things to be a true Rotarian, I would fume with anger and stop being a Rotarian because there certainly are many better ways to be. I am afraid I may be perceived as believing my way of thinking is better than someone else's, and as a result, I might do more harm than good.

At this point, I do not know how you have perceived my letters or how they have affected your life. After our club initiated a journey of 100% Paul Harris Fellow Club in July 2008, these have been a few accomplishments since five months later.

- Over $45,000 dollars were contributed to the Rotary Foundation.
- 38 members became Paul Harris Fellows compared to having two in the previous year.
- There are 22 Sustaining Members working toward Paul Harris Fellows.
- We have two major donors and more than ten multi level Paul Harris Fellows.

The most exciting factor is not how much we give to the Rotary Foundation. It is our passion and our belief that we can make a difference.

- We started with 149 members and inducted 25 new members.
- Thirty three Rotarians and friends- mostly new members and their family members- went to Guatemala for the dental and medical mission trip, compared to ten last year. A new Rotarian, Grace, is from Central America and participated on a youth exchange student program when she was a high school student in her country. She has been to Guatemala for the mission trip and is now teaching Spanish to a dozen of Rotarians every week so that our mission trip can become more successful and efficient.
- Fundraising and participation of club members and their spouses for events are more than doubled.
- We have so much fun and exceptional speakers every week, and the list goes on and on.

I can feel the excitement and pride about being a Rotarian on the faces of every member. I confess my letters and my leadership have nothing to do with these changes because the changes come from within, and I owe much of the club's success to all members. Did I make a dent in one member? I might have, and it was worth staying up late and making a connection to that person.

I no longer fight with a faceless ghost while I am writing my letters. I now have a secret admirer, and my letter from now on is for that person. You have a very special person in your heart and want to give a secret gift to her. You spend days and nights thinking about her and what to give. You secretly place it in her room, and a warm and loving feeling begins to swirl around you as you are thinking about how happy you are, having someone to admire and to give to. Hiding behind the curtain, you watch her open your gift to her, and all you can see is her smile. Haven't you given such a gift to someone that it makes you happy, just thinking about it? You do not remember what gift you gave, but you never forget the time you spent for her and her smile.

Gifts of the Magi is one of the short stories written by O. Henry. It is Christmas Eve, and Della has only one dollar and eighty-seven cents to buy a gift for her husband, Jim. They have two possessions that they cherish and take great pride in, "One was Jim's gold watch that had been his father's and his grandfather's. The other was Della's hair." Della sells her beautiful hair to buy a chain for husband's watch, and Jim sells his watch to buy Della's combs. They are "two foolish children" and "unwisely sacrificed for each other the greatest treasures," but their love for each other will be cherished and remembered forever. O. Henry concludes, "Of all who give and receive gifts, such as they are the wisest."

At first, I wanted to change you, encourage you, and inspire you through my letters. It is ironic that it was I who was changed, encouraged, and inspired while I was writing to my secret admirer. Metaphorically, all of you have been my secret admirers and always will be!

Writing has a healing power to my body and my soul; it allows me to visit places I lived in once before but have forgotten in my memory. Visiting my past has not been all beautiful, joyful, and good; I am welcome, but at the same time, I regret when I am enforced to revisit the forbidden places I want to erase from my memory. The pain that I have caused people is too deep and has left inerasable scars to be forgiven. I wish I could go back and restore it all as it was and apologize to those I hurt so much, but I can't. I have been praying for forgiveness and have apologized a thousand times, but I can't restore what was already done yesterday, last year, or ten, twenty, and thirty years ago. Even if I could make everything as beautiful, joyful, and good as it was, I do not want to change the course of my past because I might end up somewhere else other than right here, with you.

Instead of living in the past with regret and pain, I am going to live for today. In my remaining hours, I want to make ugliness beautiful, give darkness light, and fill my past with the present so that I can live in the moment. 2 Timothy 4:7 says, "I have fought the good fight, I have finished the race, I have kept the faith." I still have a strong will to fight, I will not give up until it is over, and I stake my whole life on faith.

Is the Bird Alive or Dead?

I've studied now Philosophy
And Jurisprudence, Medicine,
And even, alas! Theology
All through and through with ardour keen!
Here now I stand, poor fool…

In Goethe's Faust

A young man studied all knowledge ranging from medicine to philosophy to religion to law, but his eagerness toward his knowledge was never fulfilled. The more he studied the more he realized he was getting further away from the truth. One day, he heard from a traveler that there lived a wise man in a shabby hut on a nearby mountain. He wanted to fill his emptiness with the wise man's wisdom that can predict the future and know the fate of all beings, thus took a journey to the mountain. On his way to see the wise man he found a little bird alongside the wooden area. He carefully picked it up and put it in his pocket.

Arriving at the wise man's hut, the wise man confirmed that there was a bird in the young man's closed palm. The young man asked, "Is the bird in my hand alive or dead?" If the wise man said the bird was alive, he would squeeze the bird and kill him. If the wise man said that the bird was dead, he would simply open his hand and set him free. The young man smiled at the thought that the wise man was trapped. The young man asked him again in haste, "Is the bird in my hand alive or dead?" The wise man closed his eyes for a second; then he responded, "The faith of the bird is in your hand as the fate of your life is in your hands. Open your heart, young man, and let yourself live."

Knowledge in our head is not only useless but also blinds us from seeing the simple truths in life, if we only try to attain knowledge without putting it into action. Otherwise, knowledge is no more than what we voraciously collect, hoping it may bring happiness and believing the bumper sticker, "One who has the most toys win." Knowledge comes with responsibility. The more knowledge we have, the more responsibilities we must take on. Our heads know that a drop of vaccine costs as little as 60 cents, and it saves a child from polio, but it is our heart that takes an action and moves the mountain for them.

The Rotary Foundation received 100 million dollars, the largest grant in its 103 year history, from the Bill and Melinda Gates Foundation. Bill Gates says, "The extraordinary dedication of Rotary members has played a critical role in bringing polio to the brink of eradication. Eradicating polio will be one of the most significant public health accomplishments in history, and we are committed to helping reach that goal." It is up to you to kill polio and set our children free from it. As the fate of that bird was in the hand of the young man, so was his fate; he would open his heart and let himself live freely. The time is now. If not now, then when?

Success of our club goal depends entirely on you. All team captains and co-captains are Paul Harris Fellows, past presidents, or leaders of our club. It truly is my pleasure working with such dedicated Rotarians. Your commitment to the Rotary mission and our club goal becomes apparent as you encourage and motivate your team members to reach 100% Paul Harris Fellow Club.

I am having a difficult time expressing my true feelings in words because I am not that good at it. I want you to know I truly appreciate you taking your busy personal life, business, and family time to help others. Your dedication to Rotary and your attitude of "Service Above Self" are role models to all of us.

Rotary's goal is clear: finish the job and secure a polio-free world for all children once and for all. Please join me celebrate our 40th anniversary by becoming 100% Paul Harris Fellow Club.

One Life to Live

As I am driving home tonight after the heated Paul Harris Fellow team meeting, instead of feeling discouraged and disappointed, I am actually so proud of being a Rotarian. There were many contrary opinions and different points of views, and we obviously did not agree on everything, but one thing was clear: we love Rotary, we all have a passion for changing the lives of others, and we never lose sight of respecting one another.

Helen Keller said, "Life is a daring adventure or nothing." It does not matter how difficult our financial situations are at home or how difficult it is to give a thousand dollars to help others. It is nothing compared to children who have to live with crippled legs and damaged dignity the rest of their lives or the parents who witness firsthand the death of their sons and daughters in their arms; we fail to do what we are supposed to do as human beings.

Thirty thousand children under the age of five die everyday due to preventable causes. Even if we execute all the possible ways there is to save our children, some will still die, but not from poliovirus. They might die from not wearing helmets while riding bicycles, lack of nutrition, pneumonia, or other disease, but they will not die from poliovirus once it is completely eradicated.

I have one life to live. If I only get to live by the end of my presidency (June 2009), I asked myself one question: what is the one thing I want to do before I die? I want to love and have passion for everything I do at home, at work, and at Rotary. I want to touch every corner of this universe.

Someone said, "I expect to pass through this world but once. Any good therefore that I can do, or any kindness that I can show to any fellow creature, let me do it now. Let me not defer or neglect it, for I shall not pass this way again." I believe the person I see at this moment and whom I am thinking of is the most important person. Also, I believe the most important time is right now, the most important work is what I am doing now, and the most important way is to live by the Rotary motto, "Service Above Self" until my time on this earth ends.

I wasn't born with a burning passion for life within me. I learned it from you, ordinary Rotarians who do the extraordinary, and it has been very contagious to anyone whose life you have touched. Regardless of the outcome in June 2009, my heart and respect for you will always be unchanged because I know we did the best we could with what we had.

I do know that we will be disappointed by a few members who refuse to be Paul Harris Fellows, but I understand that their circumstances do not permit them to be at this time. My disappointment in a few members will not stop me from loving them, respecting them, and believing they will be Paul Harris Fellows once their circumstances are changed.

Philosopher and poet Johann Wolfgang von Goethe once said, "Treat people as though they were what they ought to be, and you will help them become what they are capable of becoming." We have to believe they join the Rotary for what Rotary stands for and want to be true Rotarians. Even if they give up on themselves, we will not and should not give up on them. As I close my eyes and get ready for tomorrow, I just want you to know I love you guys. Have a good night.

Wheels in Motion and COMPASS

"I have learned that people will forget what you said, people will forget what you did, but people will never forget how you made them feel."
Maya Angelou

Even though I was a new member when I joined in 2000, I was familiar with Rotary and eagerly anticipating future Rotary projects. In the back of the Gazette, Four Avenues of Service were listed along with many committees. It was both exciting and startling to see so many opportunities to serve and be a part of something great, while I was waiting for seasoned Rotarians to invite me along with other new members to club activities Several club projects were planned and carried out successfully without me. I felt I was left out but assumed that committee members were already selected and given assignments according to their past experiences and seniority in the club. I also thought new members had to be asked, so I waited for my turn to participate.

I waited a few months, and those months turned into a year. While I was waiting, club Rotarians went to Guatemala for a dental mission trip. I was getting comfortable with my role as a member. I attended the meetings, sat at the same corner tables with the same faces every week, ate breakfast, and listened to the speakers absent-mindedly. Then, I went to my workplace with a sense of emptiness, week in and week out. Groucho Marx said, "I refuse to join any club that would have me as a member." I wanted to be a Rotarian, not merely a member. My father used to say whatever you do, do it with enthusiasm and never give up. I thought being only a member was giving up my duty and my right as a Rotarian. As my desire to be a Rotarian was fading away, I was becoming more and more a mere member as the year went by.

It happened at last. Mike Fussell approached me after a club meeting and said, "Our golf tournament needs your help. The committee chair person is Joanna Blauw. Why do not you ask her how you can help?" I remember what the late Hank Thompson said to me, "I am a sign guy." Hank Thompson, Eric Jackson, and Bob Barker asked me to come to the Country Hills Golf Club at six in the morning with a hammer, and we put up twenty six signs for sponsors on 19 holes that year. The grass was so wet with early morning dew that we slid down the slope a few times and laughed at each other's butts covered with mud.

Thanks to Mike, that was how I got involved with my first Rotary project. If I wasn't asked to participate, face to face, I probably would have become a comfortable RNO (Rotarian Name Only.) I learned from my experience that approaching new members one on one and getting them involved as soon as they join is the best way to keep them for life. If we do not, we may not lose them, but they surely will remain RNO. They will pay dues, come to meetings, sit at the same tables with the same faces and eat breakfast.

Any Rotary Clubs that are full of RNO are destined to fail, or they become social clubs that have nothing to do with Rotary. We were "Service Above Self" when Paul Harris started Rotary in 1905. That is what we still are, and as long as there is one Rotarian in this world, the Rotary's Motto and action for humanity will continue forever. Also, as long as there are RNO in any club or organization, potential members or qualified workers will not join or work for organizations, and not only will RNO run off all Rotarians or dedicated workers, but they will also never leave because they think there's nothing wrong with just being a member and doing nothing.

Jim Collins argues in his book, *Good to Great*, that instead of setting a new vision and strategy for organizations, "good-to-great" leaders invest in people first. We know the old saying, "People are your most important asset," but he protests that the right people are most important to a great organization. Great leaders first have the right people get on the bus and give them the right seats; then, let the wrong people get off the bus. Once the right people have the right seats on the bus, the organization is equipped to take off to the next level. The right people believe that their organization is greater than the sum of their individuals, and they are focused and driven to success. Ken Kersey said, "There are going to be times we can't wait for somebody. Now, you're either on the bus or off the bus." I am glad to have been given the opportunity to choose between living actively as a Rotarian and simply existing as a member.

Four or five years later, Mike was the president of the COMPASS Board of directors, and our new member, Kara Arnold, was the Executive Director. I knew little about COMPASS, but Mike's leadership and more than two dozen Rotarians being COMPASS partners ensured me that I needed to get involved with this non-profit organization as well.

COMPASS is an acronym for Community Outreach Making Partnerships at Sumner Schools. The hospital I work in is a COMPASS partner with Vena Stuart Elementary. Its mission is to build the bridge between the business community and Sumner County public schools to improve student success through the gifts of time, money, and resources. The school is located where the majority of families live under poverty level and low income brackets. Approximately 75% receive a federal free and reduced meal program at the school. Since our hospital is only a couple of blocks away, many of my co-workers live nearby and send their children to the same school they graduated from.

The Gallatin Noon Rotary Club started Wheels in Motion in Gallatin public schools to build relationships with the children of our community, our future Rotarians. The mission of Wheels in Motion seems to coincide with COMPASS. Employees in my department had a difficult time serving as mentors because the key mentoring time—lunch time—is a bad time for employees who staff the cafeteria and prepare and serve lunches to patient rooms. Because of this dilemma, I chose to participate in a different way. Each month, employees pool their money and donate a bicycle to one Vena Stuart student. The school has a committee to select an outstanding individual who exemplifies good citizenship. The student is then presented the bike in front of all the students in their gym.

As a leader of my department, I want to lead my employees by example. I truly believe winning their heart is the utmost importance. I want to lead them to the next level and make them realize they have the potential to do anything they want with their lives, using the God-given talents and strengths to be successful. I simply want my employees to be happy at work because they want to be there, not because they are forced to work pay check to pay check. They have to bring out the winning attitudes within themselves that they haven't known they had before.

Leaders cannot make employees do things they do not want to do if we want to keep talented employees and develop them to be the leaders of our organization. On the other side of the wall was everything they were seeking. Some will dash to follow trusted leaders at all costs because they believe in them, some will hesitate but eventually follow the crowd, and some will not only refuse to follow, but block our path no matter what others are doing. It is the leaders' responsibility to let those who do not want to be on the same bus get off and to help them find another bus in which they can contribute. In this case, letting members off the bus do both us and them a favor.

It is important to create an environment in which creativity is encouraged, the impossible is possible, and dreams do come true. In that kind of working environment, employees are happy, learn to grow, and bloom to be the next leaders. In order for a flower to blossom, we must have both the right soil and the right seed. I identified that Wheels in Motion would create the environment that I envisioned and both my employees and students would benefit from each other and make a difference in the life of one another.

When I started Wheels in Motion for my department in 2006, many doubted what one dollar would do to make a difference in the life of a student. Many refused to give a dollar a month and did not even want to participate when I asked them to go with me to present a bike. Later I found out many genuinely wanted to contribute to society but did not know how to help because they hadn't been given such an opportunity as this to serve others, and most lived under financial constraint to get by, week by week. They saw themselves as victims and treated themselves as unworthy and invaluable. I reminded them that even if we wrinkle up, spit at, and step on a hundred dollar bill, the value of the money never decreases or changes; it is still a hundred dollar bill! It did not matter whether they are high school dropout dish washers or surgeons. Their positions, wealth, and education have nothing to do with their uniqueness and value as human beings. Human beings cannot be devalued and chained to their environment unless they give themselves away. Danny Thomas summarizes, "All of us are born for a reason, but all of us do not discover why. Success in life has nothing to do with what you gain in life or accomplish for yourself. It's what you do for others."

As I took three or four employees at a time to present a bike in front of 720 students, change was slowly taking place in those who did not believe even they could make a difference. Martin Luther King, Jr. said, "Everybody can be great…because anybody can serve. You do not have to have a college degree to serve. You do not have to make your subject and verb agree to serve. You only need a heart full of grace. A Soul generated by love." While the principal was reading a letter submitted by a teacher about why his or her student deserved to win a bike, parents who did not realize they had such precious children, and my employees who had refused to give money, were so moved that we all cried together many times in front of the poor but innocent children.

In December of last year, I challenged all students to have dreams and work hard to achieve them. In the following month, I received over 150 letters from students telling me what their dreams were in words and pictures. I brought them to my department and challenged that every student who sent us letters would receive letters in return. When I took them back to the school, the principal and teachers were completely shocked. They hadn't thought we cared enough to write letters to each and every student and wiped away their tears with awe.

I had our youth exchange student Wencke present a bike one month. She spoke about Germany and experiences as a youth exchange student in America and encouraged them to go abroad when they were in high school. Not everybody will be given the opportunity to study and learn a different culture while living in a foreign country, but some will have a dream and one day their dreams may come true, and they will have the journey of a life time. I think they were inspired to have dreams that they never dreamed before.

As I am thinking about Doran and an impetuous transformation of her life caused by tragedy, I can't help but believe that everything is a miracle, and everything happens for a reason. My heart is too overwhelmed to continue this letter, not by the tragedy that almost took her life, but by Doran's act of kindness and of love for those children. Her unforgotten act of love for the student whom she might never see again exemplified her attitude toward life and her renewed faith in God. It is her remarkable story that is encouraging me to go on.

As I watched Doran presenting a bike to a little girl, I had a flashback that took me back to two previous months before when she had a car accident on the night of Thanksgiving Day. I remembered it like yesterday when I received a phone call from a nurse. She said that my youth exchange student got involved in a car accident and was freighted in a helicopter to Vanderbilt Trauma Center. I immediately asked, "which one?" There was a 15 year old German student, Wencke and a 21 year old Korean college student, Doran, staying with me at the time. I did not know which girl she meant. After I got to the hospital, it was Doran. She had serious injuries on her head and face. As soon as I saw her lying in bed unconscious and bandaged, I collapsed to the floor and cried uncontrollably.

She was a recipient of a Rotary Cultural Ambassadorial Scholarship and came from my native country, Korea, to study English for six months in Nashville. I gladly accepted my responsibility as her host counselor when District Governor Rufus Clifford asked me to, even though I had Wencke staying with me already. I was told that our club's involvement and my responsibility for her was very limited since she was to attend language school in Belmont University and was to live in a home stay nearby the school. Also, all associated expenses were already paid by the Rotary Foundation, and transportation and meals were provided by home stay. I was there to assist her just in case the need might arise. It was a piece of cake or so I thought.

She missed Korean food and wanted to spend weekends with my family and Wencke. I picked her up on Fridays to spend weekends together, then dropped her off at her home stay in Antioch after attending church on Sundays. She was very good with my three teenagers. Having only a younger sister in Korea, she enjoyed rough and boyish play with my kids, and I know all of my three kids loved her very much. My wife and I treated her like a relative. But it changed drastically when I saw her lying in bed in a coma; I had to be her father.

Somehow I humbly thanked God in prayer for sending Doran into my life and for letting me be the one taking care of her at the worst situation. If it was meant to happen and if it was God's will, I gladly accepted my responsibility, and I was thankful for being used and chosen by the higher power. It was one of the hardest things for any parent to do, waking her own parents at three in the morning over the phone to announce the news from thousands of miles away. I honestly did not know how and what to say. I kept thinking in my mind about if that actually happened to my own daughter in a foreign country and how I should handle such news over the phone. All I could do was apologize to her parents for what happened, and her mother fainted during the phone conversation. I was able to calm her father down saying, "She is my daughter, and I will do all I can to take good care of her." Then, I promised him that I would not let her die.

It had been a long journey to recovery since then, and Doran and her mother stayed in my house for three more months. The end of February Doran was to leave for Korea. What would be the most memorable gift that I could give? I wanted her to experience what a little gift of giving meant to a student in Vena Stuart Elementary. I took her to the school to present a bike, and she wore a hat to disguise her scars on her head and face; then she gave a speech.

I am sorry for not remembering what she said to the students, teachers, and my employees in the gym. All I can remember now is her smile. Someone once said that everyone you meet deserves to be greeted with a smile however difficult your own life is. If they had known what she had to go through to be there; then, they would appreciate her genuine smile on her scarred face. On the way home Doran asked me when the next bike day was. I told her the date, which was the week before she was to leave America.

A fellow Rotarian, Debbie Lamberson, is the president of the Christmas for Kids nonprofit organization. She invited Doran and her mother to Wal Mart in December, and Robin Williams and I helped Doran shop for Christmas gifts. Her organization paid $175 for each of her four family members, and she also gave Doran a gift card so she could purchase medicine and things she needed.

Doran asked me if she could take some of her Christmas gifts back to Wal Mart and exchange them for a bike. It was her gifts from Debbie, our true Rotarian, but seeing her eyes I could not deny her sincerity and love for a student. Furthermore, it would have been an insult to her if I bought a bike for her myself. She picked out the most expensive bike and a helmet. She asked, "Do you think he would like this bike?" It was the best bike anybody could own. A day before she was to head back to Korea, I received a gift and a package of binded letters from a boy's teacher and his classmates. It was her biggest gift of all, and those little children stole her heart.

I gave her my last letter at the airport right before she took off and told her to read it on the airplane. After I returned home, I found her own letter next to her bed. Neither of us could say nor show our heart and gratitude toward each other the night before. What I did was what I was supposed to do as any parents that love their children unconditionally. This is who we are and what we do as Rotarians. However, what she did for a student at Vena Stuart Elementary was extraordinary. As she was nearing death, she chose to live a fuller life and touched many people around her.

I read a story about an Interactor Ashley Kaimowits (1985-2005) in Rotarian magazine. She lived a very short life and said, "Life of one if helped, can change the course of the world, as you never know who that one little girl or boy could be." I expect that there will be many unbeatable obstacles and unbearable tragedies tomorrow. But today, I am going to find happiness in the small things such as giving a bike to a student, for his smile is worth fighting for and overcoming all tragedy even if the tragedy takes my life away. It is worth fighting for.

Blame or Accept

When a bad thing happens to a good person, he has two choices: to blame or to accept. The attitude of blame leads him to failure because he chooses to dwell in the past with baggage on his head holding him hostage from moving forward. It is in the past. He cannot do anything about it; what is done is done. He believes that he is a failure because bad things happen to him. He blames the environment and everybody else but himself.

For example, an opposing team in a soccer game found a hole in the line and went through it without difficulty, over and over again. His team got beaten so badly that he looked for the fault in his teammates; his team lost because the hole in the line was him! It does not matter how many times he falls or how ridiculously people laugh at him, or even how he sees himself defeated and demoralized. None of those things make him a failure because no single incident can color or label his view of himself. It does not hurt if he does not let it. In other words, when people throw all kinds of baggage at him, he does not have to catch or carry it with him; acknowledge it and just let it go. He needs not to make it his own. It is not failure if he learns from his mistakes and never gives up trying to move forward.

On the contrary, the attitude of acceptance leads him to success in life. He acknowledges that all of us have experienced such incidents in our lives; he accepts it as a fact of life and uses it as a stepping stone rather than avoiding it or blaming it. John C. Maxwell, a great leader and motivator, argues in his book, "The difference between average people and achieving people is their perception of and response to failure." He continues, "The process of achievement comes through repeated failures and the constant struggle to climb to a higher level."

Looking back, every defining moment in my life that made me who I am now is due to adversity, failure, and rejection. Not a single achievement, praise, or position contributed to having a positive attitude about life or helped me find my identity and place on this earth.

Have you ever seen a flower called Man Chu Kuk? The Man Chu Kuk shuts its buds while all other flowers are busy in and out of bloom. Then, it shoots out buds in full bloom during the late, fiercely cold winter, after having endured all hardship. Even flowers possess their own beauty and imperfections, but Man Chu Kuk blooms in accordance with the looker's state of mind; it blooms with the exact color, aroma, and beauty as to please the looker's heart. It cannot be seen to those who give up trying and plump down on the ground because of momentary failure and a setback.

Robert Frost sums up life in three words, "I can sum up everything I have learned about life. It goes on." It does not matter how difficult and how painful life is, we cannot turn our backs on life because life is meant to be lived. In reality, when we are no longer defeated and rejected, we need to check our pulse; we may be walking, but dead inside! Therefore, we should welcome all obstacles and failures for encouraging us to try harder and challenging us to live to the fullest. "To achieve your dream," said John C. Maxwell, "You must embrace adversity and make failure a regular part of your life. If you're not failing, you're probably not really moving forward." I say, "You are breathing, but dead inside; you are a dead man walking."

When someone says that life is easy, I want to punch him in the mouth, not for taking life seriously, but for deceiving his own life and toying around with the precious lives of others. Life is hard. If we seek an easy life we should be born as a day-fly or a clam. Goethe said in *The Sorrows of Young Werther*, "Once we are lost unto ourselves, everything else is lost to us. I swear there are times when I wish I could be a day labourer, simply in order to have something to look forward to in the day ahead, a sense of purpose, hope." God created man in his own image and to have man rule over every living creature and everything that has the breath of life in it (Genesis 2:27-30.) We are his offspring.

Does what I am doing today truly make a difference in people's lives? If our plans and purposes in life are wrong, it is a natural course for us to fail quicker in life. Everything we created under this misassumption is a disappearing bubble in an ocean. However, if our purpose in life is to live a meaningful life moment by moment and to serve others, then we will prevail in the end as God promises.

We must not be discouraged and disappointed by our purpose not being met. We might not see Man Chu Kuk this winter, but our children will see the most beautiful flowers so as to please their hearts because we plant and fertilize the seed for them. So, the question is not whether we fail or not. It is how we are going to respond: to blame or to accept.

It All Began With S.T.

"If a man hasn't discovered something that he will die for, he isn't fit to live."

Martin Luther King, Jr.

An old monk and his disciple were traveling and came to a riverside. Heavy rain from the night caused the river to rise, and a beautiful woman was stranded and anxiously pacing up and down the riverside. The woman cried for their help, "I cannot cross the water." His disciple approached her and said that he had taken a vow of chastity, and he could not help her. The old monk picked her up and carried her to the other side of the river without hesitation, and then he hurried off as if nothing had happened. One hour passed, then two hours passed; finally they arrived at their temple by nightfall. The disciple could not stand it any longer and rebuked the old monk, "Buddha taught us not to think about a woman, let alone touch a woman. Isn't it that we monks are to keep ourselves free from contact with women? Why did you carry her across the river?" The old monk responded, "I picked her up, carried her across the river, and left the woman at the riverside. Why are you still carrying her?"

A few days later, the old monk had to go to the village to beg for food from door to door for his daily ritual. He arrived at the riverside again, and as a pool of water began to flow off, he found a precious stone in the bottom of the river. He continued his journey and met a beggar who was shabbily dressed and had nothing to eat. He opened his bag, shared his food with the beggar, and gave him the precious stone without any hesitation. The beggar rejoiced at his sudden good fortune, for this precious stone would provide him and his family with riches and security for a lifetime.

The next morning, the beggar came to the temple to see the old monk and return the precious stone. He said, "You know how valuable the precious stone was, but you gave it to a total stranger as if it was nothing valuable. Instead of this precious stone, please give me your heart that treats a precious stone as a rock, and teach me your heart that enables you to help a hungry man when you have little."

Last month, I mailed my presumably last letter promoting and encouraging 100% Paul Harris Fellow Club. I only know one way to write, and that is to speak from my heart. The author, Saint-Exupery, says in *The Little Prince*, "It is only with the heart that one can see rightly; what is essential is invisible to the eye." I have not known any other way but to be naked in complete truthfulness and honesty in front of you, even if the whole world laughs at my nakedness. I have to be my true self rather than disguise myself as someone I am not.

Conveying true feelings, making a fictitious story, or even beautifying ugliness are not simple tasks, but somehow any good writer and good motivator can create greatness over simplicity. We cry, laugh, and applaud for their skillful mastery in penmanship. If readers are not motivated to take action, the author's penmanship is wasted and useless.

It is not easy to be a great Rotarian, but there are many ways to become one. If my letters convince one member to quietly go out and march for "Service Above Self," I believe the member is transformed into a Rotarian for life, and other

Rotarians will see why we are proud of ourselves for eradicating polio and will themselves become Paul Harris Fellows. Rotary was one man's idea in 1905; all revolutions are one man's thought at first. When one member starts to march for a Paul Harris Fellow, I do believe the rest of us will follow in his footsteps. "This, then, is the test we must set for ourselves: not to march alone, but to march in such a way that others will wish to join us," said Hubert Humphrey.

My letters are probably read by my club members since I put it in their faces every month but in reality, I am writing to my three children: Doun, Hannie, and Ahrahm. Viktor Frankl was arrested and taken to a concentration camp. He witnessed his father die of starvation, his mother and brother be killed, and his wife die at Bergen-Belsen in 1945. He survived and left the following words in *Man's Search for Meaning*. "At any moment, man must decide, for better or for worse, what will be the monument of his existence. …everything can be taken from a man but one thing: the last of the human freedoms—to choose one's attitude in any given set of circumstances, to choose one's own way."

I want my children to see how I have lived my life and want them to know not only that I stand for something great but that I also have acted on it. Also, I want them to see how much I enjoy being a Rotarian. If I can make my children understand that Rotary has helped me discover my place in this world, ignite my passions for life, and totally commit to "Service Above Self," my mission is complete.

I thought I had nothing left to say at this point because the ones who are willing to see, hear, and speak have already seen, heard, and spoken about your passion for being Rotarians and what it means to be Paul Harris Fellows. In fact, most of you initiated the first step toward Paul Harris Fellows by becoming

Sustaining Members and are encouraging others to do so. Thank you very much for giving your wealth and your heart.

Looking back, I was a disciple who was blind to see the truth that all teaching and knowledge should lead us to virtuous action and the beggar who carries a precious stone in me. Someone said, "If you have much, give of your wealth; if you have little, give of your heart." Today, I want you to meet a Rotarian sitting next to you each week who lives by the principle and gave me a precious stone without hesitation. At first, he became my friend, my mentor and now he is my true hero. If it wasn't for this Rotarian, I'd probably still be waiting to be asked to be a member today, and I would not realize I was born with wings to soar into the sky and envision creating a better world. Thanks to S.T., I not only belong to such a fine Rotary club, but I have also found a meaningful life through the fellowship I share with him, Mary Ann and other Rotarians. Most of all, his unremembered acts of kindness and of love are the role model to all of us, and I am very thankful for him bridging me to the Rotary world I had never known.

The first Rotary Club in Korea was chartered in 1927. Today the membership has grown to be the fourth largest, and its financial contribution to the Rotary Foundation is the third largest in the world followed by the U.S. and Japan. Having the first Korean Rotary International President for 2008-2009 is not a coincidence; it is more than just an honor to Dong Kurn Lee himself but a historical event for over 200 Rotary countries. Growing up in Korea, I witnessed the enormous achievements and legacy that Rotary Clubs were making. I envied the characters of Rotarians who were role models and served above themselves on behalf of their communities and the rest of the world.

All modern Presidents of South Korea had been Rotarians, and the best and selective people from the privileged classes were chosen to be members of the most prestigious Rotary Clubs. The possibility of me being a member in Korea was beyond my wildest dreams and imagination; unless I held a powerful and influential position in Korea along with having a high ethical standard. Since there were no Interact Clubs, I had to settle with Boy Scouts, instead. It holds true to many other countries. For example, when we were in Guatemala for our Rotary mission trip several years ago, Marco, our host Guatemalan Rotarian, asked us to go to his friend's house for a birthday party. When we arrived it was the house of the Vice President of Guatemala. We had a great time and never imagined we would get to celebrate a birthday with his family. It only happens in Rotary!

Facing the reality of Rotary Clubs in Korea, I misconceived that it had to be more difficult to join in the U.S, the birth place of Rotary. I joined other civic organizations and was actively involved with the community I lived in. As much as I kept myself busy with volunteering, my heart was getting empty and began to lose interest because I felt I was forced to join for my own selfish reason: business recognition, my own reputation, and networking. After all, it was not Rotary.

Occasionally I met people wearing a Rotary emblem and asked with broken English, "Please invite me to your club. I want to be a Rotarian." My roar to be a Rotarian became an echo within their laughter until S.T. abruptly showed up in my restaurant with a folded newspaper in his hand. At that time, I had just graduated from a leadership program in Nashville area. There were several Rotarians among the leadership alumni and my classmates, but I still wonder to this day why they never asked me to join. Well… S.T. came when I had officially given up and did not care for joining Rotary.

He demanded to see the owner, and when I approached him, he abruptly pointed at the newspaper article and said, "What is wrong with this article?" I had a full page ad with my brief personal story and a list of organizations that I belonged to. At first, I was offended by his remark because people had told me how nice the article was. How dare a gray haired stranger with a funny last name-Womeldorf-appear out of the blue and ask what was wrong with my newspaper article!

He appeared as if he did not care about my irritated facial expression toward him. He immediately continued saying that there was no mention of the Rotary club in my article. He said, pointing proudly at the yellowish Rotary pin on his shirt, "I want to invite you to the Hendersonville Rotary club." Without my approval he told me he would come next Wednesday morning at seven to pick me up. Half shocked and half absent minded, I responded, "What took you guys so long?"

I was happy and wasn't concerned that all one hundred and twenty plus members except myself were Caucasian. It really made me cry with pride within myself when Bill Taylor announced me as a new member and S.T. pinned the Rotary emblem on my shirt for the first time in my life. I think that year, S.T. brought more than a dozen new members. Does he have a secret recipe? Yes, he does. He simply asks, asks, and asks potential or qualified prospective members and refuses to accept the answer "no." My fellow Rotarians, I have to ask you this. Would you invest your time, money, and effort to someone like me who is waiting for an invitation and whom you think would make a great Rotarian? S.T. did!

My friend, John Christopher, is a famous, aged artist. He gave me a few of his original paintings and wrote me the following letter.

I had a tough time choosing what painting to give to you. One of my favorite water colors that I did, awhile ago, is a subject that I always like. It is the "emotional colors" of rushing waters, and the power of the rocks, protecting the glorious trees in the background; those trees I made into shapes like flowery bushes. It looks like God himself trimmed them with such accuracy, and the pines that are behind the trees keep the harsh winds in winter time from any frost bite, for in nature itself, there always seems to be an order of natural security, where if left by itself, it can last for a thousand years.

Nature may look to the unknowing human eyes to be chaotic with bushes and rocks tossed about as if God did not care. However, it takes keen observation to see the birds that control the insects, and the tougher trees in front of the blossomed trees, for each item in nature is there to take care of itself.

Even a worthless rock and a tree in nature have reasons to be there and a season to change. I truly believe each and every human being has a reason to be here and are given specific responsibilities to play an important role in the human race. Edwin Hubbel Chapin said, "Every action of our lives touches on some chord that will vibrate in eternity." In my first letter, I expressed my belief that it really does not matter how small my life is compared to someone else who contributed more greatly such as Abraham Lincoln or Mahatma Gandhi.

I wonder what would happen to Abraham Lincoln or Mahatma Gandhi. Would they have been remembered as some of the greatest men in the world and have accomplished such remarkable achievements for the world and people in their countries, if Abraham Lincoln was born somewhere in a remote village in Africa or Mahatma Gandhi in a busy street of America? Mahatma Gandhi said, "I have nothing new to teach the world. Truth and nonviolence are as old as the hills. All I have done is to try experiments in both on as vast a scale as I could." I do not think his sustaining ideology could have been easily accepted by materialized American and European culture.

Bill Gates Sr. said, "If my son had been born in sub-Saharan Africa, there would be no Microsoft, no Bill & Melinda Gates Foundation. In an ideal world, every child, regardless of the circumstances of birth, would have the opportunity to live up to his or her full potential."

I am grateful for S.T. for recognizing the potential in people's hearts and creating the environment so that people like me could use our God given talents. Every human being is worthwhile in telling his own story. Let me tell you how S.T. touched me and unknowingly made a difference in someone else's life through me.

Before I opened up my own restaurant in Hendersonville, I worked at the Cock of the Walk Restaurant in Nashville for 12 years as a bus boy, dishwasher, cook and waiter, where I successfully worked my way to the top as a general manager. As you lead your organizations, you know that a leader requires many responsibilities unrelated to what you do at work. There were about ten Spanish speaking employees from Mexico and Guatemala out of eighty employees. For some reason I felt a strong urge to help them because I was responsible for their well being and the quality of their life as long as they worked for me.

I remember how long it took me to order simple meals at McDonald's by myself. Numbered combo meals did not exist on the menu at that time. Since I could not pronounce "medium" or "large," I always had to have a small drink and eat small sizes; I had to order only what I could pronounce correctly or point to the picture. For example, I went to a movie theater and said, "I want to see 'Furee Weary.'" The cashier kept asking me which movie, and I repeated "Furee Weary." This exchange went for awhile, and both of us got so frustrated at one another. I thought I pronounced the word correctly, and the cashier obviously thought I was too dumb and too ignorant to pick a movie I wanted to see. Finally the cashier told me angrily to step aside, and I did not have a choice but to pick the movie I could pronounce, which was "Lion King." A guy behind me understood what I was trying to say and told the cashier, "He meant 'Free Willy!'"

I felt the problems that my employees were facing were indeed my own, and I felt pity that what they had to deal with everyday life. I decided to teach them basic English twice a week after work at their apartment. I could not convert them to telemarketers on the phone, but I at least wanted them to be able to order what they liked at restaurants and to see the movies of their choice at the theater. If they liked to eat beans and rice everyday at home, so be it. They shouldn't feel captive and chained to their environment permanently, solely because of language barriers.

Even though I enjoyed working with them, I was filled with yet another desire to continue my journey. I resigned my position as general manager and purchased my dream…my own business. Well, you know the rest of the story of what happened to my business if you have read the previous letters. To make a long story short, a former employee who was taught English by me (I call it distinguished Southern Korean-English!)

went back to Guatemala, got married and came back to Nashville with his wife and his three year old girl. He spoke very good English and was working at a high paying job in Nashville when he found me. The bad news traveled so fast, and he and his wife wanted to help my dying business. After long hours at another job and on his days off, they came to my restaurant and worked until late at night for minimum wage. Even on many off days they volunteered to come and work without pay.

Somehow I wasn't surprised at the news and had anticipated it would happen sooner or later; however, it was sudden and too soon when the landlord announced the news at my first meeting with him to close down my business without prior warning as the rent payments were delaying further behind. I owed Armando and his wife two weeks salary but did not know their new address. S.T.'s youngest daughter adopted a beautiful girl, Isabel, from Guatemala, and he told me about the mission trip to Guatemala lead by Bill Taylor, David and Diane Black, S.T. and other Rotarians.

S.T. and I talked about how I should pay back their salary and came to the conclusion that I needed to go to the mission trip with S.T. and pay the salary to the people in Guatemala since I could not otherwise pay them directly. That was how my first trip to Guatemala began, and last year my daughter who was fifteen years old at that time went with us and paid her dues that her daddy owed. I have made mission trips three times with S.T. and the Rotarians mentioned above, and some year with Rip and Pat Lebkuecher, Brenda Payne, Jason Tabor, Debbie Lamberson, and other non Rotarians. I am very thankful for their hard work, sacrifices, and especially the fellowship we shared. You are the hardest working Rotarians and best friends!

In addition, I must mention two of my special employees who met and married while both were working for me over several years. Working full time, attending college, and trying to begin a new family are not easy jobs for a newlywed young couple. I thought about what would be the best gift for them and the things they really needed that would last for a long time. After graduating from Middle Tennessee State University, the bride became an elementary school teacher, and they needed two cars to go to school and work. I had a beaten up old LTD Ford and a sports car that was driven only on weekends with the T-top on, and oh, how much I loved that car! My wife came home from work and found out I had given my sports car away with a book written by Dave Ramsey, *Financial Peace*. If you think I am telling this story to boost myself, you are absolutely mistaken. It is imperative to explain what S.T. did to my family.

After I filed bankruptcy, both my wife and I needed a job right away. Both of us landed separate jobs, and it was difficult to commute with one car. One morning S.T. came to where I worked and took me to Rotarian Bill Kemp, County Clerk office where I found out S.T. was giving me his van and changing the title to my name. The van was checked by a mechanic, an oil change was done, and it had a full tank of gas when he brought his van to me with a key. I did not know what to say or how to thank him. At that moment, I remembered the gift of a car I had given to my friends. I told him the story, and both of us just smiled at each other with a warm feeling inside because no words were needed to express my gratitude. He had read my heart already. He finally said, "What goes around comes around."

My brother-in-law was only fifty years old when he died of cancer. Since we had just moved to Hendersonville from Mount

Juliet, my wife and I had no friends to ask to babysit my three kids while we went to the funeral. The only person I could think of was, of course, S.T. S.T. was battling with prostate cancer at that time, and I told my kids that S.T. Harabugi (Grandfather) is sick so please listen to him and behave. Several years later, S.T. told me what happened that night. My youngest son, Doun, was showing off his martial art moves he just learned. His older brother, Hannie, who was about seven years old at the time, said to him, "My uncle died of cancer. My Mom and Dad are going to see him at the funeral home." S.T.'s eyes were wet with tears by the time he shared the rest of the story and continued with Hannie's statement, "I know you are sick. Are you going to die?" S.T. said no. "I do not want you to die." My son gave him a big hug. I lost my dad in July of 2007, and it really is killing me not being able to see him and talk to him. Most of all, I am saddened by my kids not having a grandfather. Having S.T. and Mary Ann around my family is such a comfort and joy. Now he is the only Harabugi to my kids. Thank you S.T. and Mary Ann for being there for my children.

From time to time, S.T. would spiritually plant a seed of bamboo tree on my family. After the seed of a bamboo is planted in the soil, you see nothing at all for the first three years, and only the planter will know he planted the seed. In the fourth year, a little shoot slowly comes out of the bulb. You still do not see any growth, but the planter knows that in the fifth year that the Korean bamboo tree grows up to 130 feet. All that time, the bamboo tree was growing underground, waiting for the time to reach the sky. That is how S.T. plants a bamboo tree on everyone he touches.

My wife and I were struggling with finances and were supporting my parents and younger brother who lived with us.

S.T. and Mary Ann are a Major Donor which means they donated over $10,000 to the Rotary Foundation. He never enforced me to donate money to the Rotary Foundation. Instead, he would mention the Polio Plus program and his trip to Guatemala and various ways to help people. Once I became a Paul Harris Fellow, thanks to Bill Sinks for his encouragement, my wife and my three children became Paul Harris Fellows as well. I think my daughter was about eleven years old when she first put her money in her Paul Harris Fellow piggy bank, and it took her three years to become a Paul Harris Fellow. It took another two more years for my two sons and my wife. They do not exactly know what and who Paul Harris Fellow is, but they are proud of their achievements because they raised $1,000 each by themselves. They have never been to India to give polio drops in the mouths of children of all ages, but they somehow know they are doing their parts in eradicating polio. I told them they are the man riding a bicycle to give out polio vaccine and the woman carrying a cooler for polio drops. If it weren't for your donations it would be impossible.

Let me share with you the life lesson of how important it is to have character rather than worry about how people perceive you or your reputation. John Wooden once said, "Be more concerned with your character than with your reputation. Your character is what you really are while your reputation is merely what others think you are." I agree with his statement.

At one of the Chamber of Commerce events, I saw one of our Rotary club members, and I was obviously very pleased to see him. He was talking to three other persons when I approached him to say hi. I guess he was too embarrassed by me to act like I was a close friend in front of his well dressed friends. He introduced me to his friends by saying, "He is just a cook." Normally it would not bother me the way I was treated and being laughed at. He was right in a sense; after all, I was an owner of a restaurant, a cook, and dish washer since I wore so many different hats. However, his tone of voice and laughter indicated they were making fun of me after all. I kept smiling and kept the dejection, hurt, and humiliation to myself, but somehow it grew bigger and bigger because I reallydid not expect that kind of treatment from a loving fellow Rotarian. Realizing I was still treated as an outsider by some members, after being a member for several years, was more than I could take. I had the highest regard and respect for Rotarians and believed that we were a different breed of people—kind, generous, and above all, Service Above Self. That incident made me realize I could never be a part of the Hendersonville Rotary family, no matter how hard I tried. I asked myself what I had to do to be accepted as a Rotarian, and the withdrawal from the club was my answer if I could not be accepted.

I made my mind to leave the club after coming back from a 10 day Guatemala mission trip with .S.T., Bill Taylor, Brenda Payne, David Black, and Cyndi Tierney from Gallatin Morning club. I intended to participate in all Rotary activities because I might not get to do what I loved so much. The night before we were headed back to Nashville from Guatemala, I told them my decision that I chose to be a Rotarian because I believed what Rotary stood for. I did not have to be a member of Rotary club to be a Rotarian. It wasn't right and fair for me to be mistreated, but they all understood why I had to leave the club and apologized to me on behalf of other members who had insulted and mistreated me.

The following month at our annual banquet I was awarded the Rotarian of the Year. I had mixed feelings and thought it was hypocritical that I was not accepted by members, but the members selected me as the Rotarian of the Year. I could not accept such an honor and did not feel as if I deserved it. I wrote my resignation letter to the club president, Todd Odum, and chose to be a Rotarian on my own and not be a member of the Rotary club. I justified that it would be like being a Christian, yet not attending church.

I terribly missed participating in the Festival by the Lake, Relay for Life, Mission Trip to Guatemala, and even weekly meetings that I had dreaded to go on some mornings and all the other things that I felt I had to do as a Rotarian. Most of all, I truly missed seeing my fellow Rotarians every week. I did not want to get up at six in the morning every three months to pick up trash on our Roadside Clean Up. I did not have to do it anymore, and I should have been happy about that. But the moment I realized I was no longer able to do those things on my own, it hit me how much fun I had with fellow Rotarians and their families and how much it meant to me. Yes, I missed even picking up trash. I no longer was able to travel to Guatemala with the most caring Rotarians and share their fellowships. Thank God that S.T. would visit me in Lebanon regularly and inform me on how our club and my friends in the Rotary club were doing, ensuring me to come back when I was ready.

My heart was broken into pieces and remained frozen as an iceberg, but S.T.'s warm heart slowly melted my frozen heart away and put the broken pieces all together. I had decided to leave because of negative comments that some members made, and it was wrong of me to make an assumption to be true, and that that was an opinion of our club as a whole. Now my heart was filled with love and friendship, and I badly wanted to come back because of one Rotarian, S.T. I realized I made a big mistake leaving the club, and I was also glad to realize how much I missed Rotary and my friends while I was gone for a year. If I stayed I would probably have remained unhappy and failed to recognize how wonderful life is with Rotary, but I especially give thanks to S.T., Bill Taylor, Robin Williams, David & Diane Black, Bob Barker, and Brenda Payne for their understanding and for standing by me when I felt the whole world was crashing down on me.

To be honest with you, I still see that member in our regular club meeting every week. He might think he degraded me, humiliated me, and devalued my worth as a human being. As a result, he wanted me to quit, but on the contrary, every time I remember what he did, it gives me strength and encouragement to be a better person. I tell myself that never again will I leave this club and my friends. If life is like building my own house, I am willing to build my house on rocks with stones and negative words that people throw at me, instead of running away from those objects. It might not be much of a pretty sight compared to a gilded house built on sand, but you are always welcome to my house.

Why should I quit now because of negative comments? I have shown courage for years and was able to stand up every time I fell. I shall not lose it so others can feel as though they defeated me. Most of all, I have many wonderful Rotary friends and a loving family who love and encourage me. That is more than enough reason to stay and fight.

Is it achievable to have 100% Paul Harris Fellow Club? I know as long as there are members who join the Rotary Club with the wrong reason and have no desire to give hope and freedom to children from polio, no such goals are possible. So, why did I set this personal goal for our club? To show there are more good and caring people in our community than the few who try to bring good people down. If good people do nothing, it means less caring people are winning. We can't let that happen. All Rotarians must stand for what is right and fight for the best interests of the good. If it weren't for S.T. and my fellow

Rotarians I admire, I would probably do nothing and let bad people walk over me.

I will do my best to meet 100% Paul Harris Fellow Club in my presidency, and if I fail to meet our club goal this year, I will try every year until the goal is met. After that, I will work on other clubs. One day all 3,300 Rotarians will be Paul Harris Fellows and all 65 clubs in our district will be 100% Paul Harris Fellow Club. However, I will never allow a 100% certificate to be the judge of our success. Whether we achieve our success depends on each of us doing the best we could when we had so little. That is more meaningful than someone contributing a million dollars to the Rotary Foundation with no concept of what Rotary is and careless about how the money is spent.

"The great essentials of life are something to do, something to love, something to hope for" said Thomas Chalmers. If it wasn't for S.T. and my fellow Rotarians I do not think I would be as passionate about what I do, how much I love Rotary, and hope for the future of our children.

The train I am in is departed with no certain place to go. I have been aboard this train for 45 years now, and it will be a very short journey to my destination; then, I have to make room for someone else when the time comes. The people I love dearly already got off, and I see new passengers getting aboard and filling their empty seats.

Whether I am a cook or street sweeper I have to get off when it is my time. I hope I can proudly say I lived my life fully, the way it was meant to be lived, and I was never an idle spectator of my own life while my train is passing by. Martin Luther King, Jr. said, "If a man is called to be a street sweeper, he should sweep the streets even as Michelangelo painted or Beethoven composed music or Shakespeare wrote poetry. He should sweep streets so well that all the hosts of heaven and earth will pause to say: Here lived a great street sweeper who did his job well."

I think it is up to us what kind of world we are leaving behind for our children, for they are the ones taking our places in the train. Yes, it will be a very short journey. I am going to live while I am alive. I am going to love while I am able to love, and I am going to forgive before I get off this train. When all the bad things happened to me I used to say, "Why me?" Our train is going so fast that we do not have time to blame ourselves nor waste time on things that we can't control. I certainly do not want to waste my last minutes on things that do not matter. Thank you S.T. and my fellow Rotarians! My life is enriched by you, and I thank you again for accepting me as a Rotarian. I want to live my life the way you live and walk the way you walk because you live and walk by the principle of my Lord, Jesus Christ.

As you already know, I hate being half done. Our goal is 100% for each and every one of you to contribute $1,000 to Paul Harris Fellow, not 50% nor 99% this year to celebrate our 40th Anniversary and to stomp on preventative Polio for good. Will we fail to reach our goal because of you? How are we going to tell children that their legs are crippled, and their brother and sister died of malnutrition and malaria because I did not do my part as a Rotarian?

"No snowflake in an avalanche ever feels responsible."
Stanislaus Lezczynski

My Mission Statement

I am a Christian (GROWTH)
    Go to God in prayer daily.
    Read God's Word daily.
    Obey God, moment by moment.
    Witness for Christ by my life and words.
    Trust God for every detail of my life.
    Holy Spirit—Allow God to control and empower my daily life.
    Learn to love and forgive.
    Go on mission.
    Go to church every Sunday.

I am a family man
I believe in God, and God loves me.
Each of us is a child of God, and all of us love our Lord with one heart.
I love my family with all my heart and respect others.
I do my best at all things, and I do not rely on others.
I will never give up no matter what.
No debt and absolutely no debt.
I am completely honest and truthful.
Life is good, and I enjoy my life.
I am thankful.
Spend one on one time with family members.
Live a healthier life.
Write a letter to loved ones every week.

I am a coach
    Be a human being.
    Be responsible for your actions.
    Be humble.

Do your duty.
Do one good deed every day.
Have a positive attitude and positive thinking.
Be proactive.
Begin with the end in mind.
Put first things first.
Think win/win.
Seek first to understand…then to be understood.
Synergize.
Sharpen the saw.

I am a student

Write my journal everyday.
Publish a book.
Read one book a week (50 books a year & 3000 books in my lifetime.)
Read the entire Encyclopedia Britannica.
Read the entire Britannica Great Books.
Read the entire Korean Dictionary.
Visit 50 States.
Visit North America.
Visit Central America.
Visit Africa.
Visit Europe.
Visit Asia.

I am a Rotarian. (Four-Way Test of the things we think, say, or do)

Is it the truth?
Is it fair to all concerned?
Will it build goodwill and better friendships?
Will it be beneficial to all concerned?

Where There Is a Will, There Is a Way

"Kim, haven't you learned your lesson yet? Whenever you make a large donation to the Rotary Foundation, you lose your job." I corrected him, "I became a Paul Harris Fellow AFTER I lost my business." "Thank God," I continued, "this time I became a Major Donor two weeks BEFORE I lost my job!" My friend and I were laughing at a strange coincidence and the difficult circumstances of when I became a Paul Harris Fellow and a Major Donor.

On July 22, 2008, I was promoted to a new position. Then, about three months later on November 4, my job along with ninety positions were let go from the hospital. At forty six year of age, I was downsized for the first time in my life; somebody else's horrifying story on the television or newspaper became my own. The reality was harsh and has not sunk in yet. It has been six weeks now; my wife is worried about how we are going to make next month's mortgage, car payments, pay utility bills, buy Christmas gifts for our three children, and most of all, get food on the table.

I, on the other hand, am anxious to find out God's plan for me and my family. Oddly enough I was excited about losing a job that I loved. I cannot help but anticipate where God will lead me from here. Everything I have done up to this moment is a building block to the next chapter of my life, and I am grateful that I am still useful in God's eye.

I have not always felt God's presence throughout my life. When I was content with my life I completely ignored God's existence. When I abandoned myself to despair, struggled with adversity, and felt a sense of alienation, I invited Him into my life without fail, and demanded Him to fix my Godless life. Furthermore, I blamed Him and pointed my fingers at other people for putting me into such chaotic and inevitable situations. I confess that was yesterday before I accepted Him as my Savior. Today I am thankful for being alive and for Him giving me an opportunity to serve Him and do His work through me.

Based on my experience, He neither failed me nor abandoned me. He has always stood by me and forgiven me, even though I failed Him, abandoned Him, and denied Him repeatedly. At the lowest point of my life, I have found God residing in me and realized I have received more than enough. I have become happier as I learn to be thankful for what I am given and richer as I am content with less possessions.

Not everyone would understand what I did was right for my family since we were on the verge of starvation if I did not find a job right away. Some will accuse me for neglecting my duty as a father and for failing to provide the best interest of my children. In addition, some will say I did it to save my face at the expense of my own family. I questioned myself again and again whether I was too blind to see which is more important between my own family and the faceless and nameless children in poor countries. I will have you answer it for yourself after you read my story about how I became a Major Donor.

While club members are contributing one thousand dollars to be Paul Harris Fellows, I set my goal of ten thousand dollars to be a Major Donor. I believed I should have a higher standard if I expected members to follow suit. Since my three children and I were already Paul Harris Fellows, I needed six thousand dollars more to meet my goal of becoming a Major Donor by June 2009.

"Where there is a will, there is a way." We hear it so often that it sounds like untruth and myth and yet, meaningless and numb to believers. I think a "way" grows in proportion as how strong is our "will" and how badly we want it. Let's return to Doran Lee's story.

When Doran was discharged from the Vanderbilt Medical Center after the horrible car accident, Doran's mouth was completely shut with wires after the surgery. She was not able to eat or speak for four to six weeks. She had to visit the hospital for medical treatments several times a week. My wife and I felt it was our responsibility to take care of her, however long it might take; so we asked her and her mother to recuperate at my house. However, Doran and her mother did not want to add anymore burdens onto my wife and me. Instead she decided to stay at Doran's home stay. My wife and I begged Doran and her mother to stay with us and receive medical care until she was fully recovered and prepared to return to Korea. We already lined up fellow Rotarians to take her to the hospital and doctor's office, and I was happy to be there to translate for her.

Our club immediately formed an ad-hoc committee to help her with finances and volunteers. It was one of those unforgettable moments that touched so many Rotarians and Rotary clubs. It brought us all together, I was so proud of being a Rotarian. I witnessed Rotarians from all walks of life praying for her, volunteering to help, and donating money to a student whom they never met.

Medical bills were accumulating innumerably, and our club decided to help her personal expenses first. Doran and her mother were to pay seven hundred dollars to their home stay every week. The problem arose the first day they moved in due to the misunderstanding of their different cultures. I immediately brought them to my house, and they lived with me for the next three months.

Our club approved to pay seven hundred dollars a week to the home stay. Therefore, it did not matter to our club where Doran and her mother stayed as money was concerned. It would cost the club the same amount of money either way. The committee persisted in paying me when they were told Doran and her mother moved in with me. I perfectly understood and would support the club's decision, if it was given to somebody else.

As far as I was concerned, she was my daughter, and I felt blessed and grateful having her and taking care of her at her crucial moment between life and death. I said to committee members, "No way in the world would I have them pay for anything while they are in my house!" As much as I argued and fought, I could not deny the club's sincerity and want to help. They wanted to be a part of helping hands by supporting me. I finally settled with one thousand dollars a month. I did not tell my wife about the money; I wasn't sure how I was going to use that money, but I made up my mind I would not use it to pay her expenses.

TI was promoted in July (if I had known then that my new position would be eliminated three months later, I would have said no thank you and ran away.) I had more than three weeks vacation built up and had a choice to take a long vacation before starting a new role. Keeping my promise and being a part of eradicating polio was a much greater need than my own and my family's pleasure. I cashed in and was reimbursed three thousand dollars.

With six-thousand dollars I could do many things to make my family happy. I could fix my kitchen floors for my wife and literally have a peace of mind from her nagging. The first year of college tuition for my daughter could be paid in full. My two teenage boys could stop complaining about why they do not have an iPod, Xbox 360, or cellular phones with unlimited text messaging like all of their friends. My car was so old and ugly even my own kids did not want me to pick them up in school, and I was driving with engine lights on and broke down in the middle of the road several times already. I needed another used car and the list goes on.

I confess that my family's dire needs appeared to be more important and urgent than saving lives of faceless and nameless children from the polio in other countries. It was difficult to thrust temptation away. I could buy them with money and be the best husband and father for a while. Also, I felt I was charged with a crime for refusing to provide the needs of my family when I could. As a matter of fact, I had every right to use my money as pleased. However, I could not escape from my conscience whispering, "Follow your heart and do what is right because conscience of none is non-human."

If you have six-thousand dollars of free money in your hand, what would you do with it, and how would you spend it? Do you still think that I should spend all that money on the wants of my family? In truth, my wife and my children do not know what I did and why they could not get what they wanted. One day I hope they will realize what is more important between the wants of my family and the needs of poor children. Would stuff we could have with six thousand dollars buy my family happiness? Would they be happier knowing that the money that should have been spent on them, actually saved twelve thousand children from polio?

I am sorry I could not provide all the things my family wanted, but I truly believe I did the right thing to save the lives of children from polio with six thousand dollars. After all, it was free money; some might disagree, but that is alright. I made Doran a Paul Harris Fellow, and she was recognized with seventeen other new Paul Harris Fellows last month.

She sent wonderful gifts to all of my family for Christmas. Making her a Paul Harris Fellow with six thousand dollars was my gift to her and my promise to all Rotarians that I am determined to do my part in eradicating the polio at all costs. We have been waiting for someone else to finish what we started, while children are dying everyday. We have been talking and preparing for what should do for years, while children are crippled everyday. I do not want somebody else to live my life for me, and neither of you. I do not want to leave it to somebody else what I was destined to do. I have to believe that it is our destiny as a Rotarian to end this, and no one but ourselves can do this. The time to act is now. Let's finish this damn thing once and for all!

Fellow Rotarians, you have not answered my question yet. What would you do if you had six-thousand dollars of free money today?

Each of us will one day be judged by our standards of life, not by our standards of living; by our measure of giving, not by our measure of wealth; by our simple goodness, not by seeming greatness.

William Arthur Ward

See You Later

Which sin is worse,
Loving someone I am not allowed to love,
Or not knowing the one who loves only me
Through all eternity?
In any event, I commit a divine sin.

The highest punishment for a man
Is death you say
For me, it is waiting
Waiting for you
I could breathe but could not
I want to die but must not
I need not love but must love you.

I was seventeen years old when I came to America. The American language, as in American life and its culture, changes constantly and makes it difficult for a youth exchange student to speak the American language and assimilate into the American culture. F.H. Lee who lived in Japan said from his life experience in his book *An English Country Calendar*, "In order to master the English language thoroughly and, consequently, to be able to really appreciate English literature, it is necessary to have a clear understanding of the Englishman's character. It is hardly sufficient to know his manner of life without seeking to find out why he thinks and acts in the way he does."

Everything seemed so foreign and displaced that there was hardly anything I was able to function in my daily life. Playing soccer for my high school team was probably the only thing connected me to the world of friendship, school, and American life; first and foremost, it literally saved me from the alienation and displacement.

I was not an exceptional soccer player as every student and my school thought I was, and I surely was not a threat to every parent and teacher because of the simple fact that I was a second degree black belt. I grew up playing soccer and learned Tae Kwon Do from an early age, just like any normal kid in Korea. It was the first year that my school started a High School soccer team, and I was the only one who knew how to play; thus, I automatically became the captain of the team and an instant soccer star.

As soon as I stepped out of my house, I not only had to face cultural and social barriers but also had to deal with problems associated with American language, ethnic minority, and discrimination, which were my biggest obstacles since I never had to deal with them in my native country. Naturally I felt helpless, vulnerable, and displaced; furthermore, I badly needed friends who could help me with my daily activities such as doing my homework, ordering what to eat at the school cafeteria, and giving me rides to and from soccer practices and games.

I truly believe it was due to mutual respect that bound us so strong from the start. I had no other way but to depend on my soccer teammates for everything, and they were my only friends that I had at the time. They eagerly adopted, protected, and treated me as their beloved mascot, a golden boy. While I saw myself different from them and tried to build the wall to protect myself from the rest, they embraced and treated me as one of their own. How could I ever thank them for accepting me as who I was and teaching adults by example, not to discriminate by the color of my skin? They slowly tore down barriers that already existed, one by one.

There was a beautiful girl in school who was blonde, popular, and friendly. She often came to watch our soccer games. I thought she came to see me because she always talked to me before and after games. She was the only girl that hung out and talked with me and my friends during breaks at school. Oh, if I had known then what I know now, I would have been her best friend and not have broken her heart! I would have gone to the prom with her, even now. I have forgotten her name, but like the end of *The Prince of Tides*, "I whisper these words: 'Lowenstein, Lowenstein.'"

As I mentioned earlier, I hung out with my teammates in the hallway in front of the library during breaks. I could not understand any of the words coming out of their mouths, but they did not care whether I understood them or not. They always included me in their conversations; I giggled when they giggled and began to imitate their behavior and their speech. As days went by, I began to feel comfortable with my friends and look forward to breaks between classes everyday. I especially looked forward to my fourth period break, not because I missed or needed my friends, but because she came to talk to us.

One day she waved her hand and said something to me as she was leaving for her classroom. I caught one of my teammates by his shoulder and asked him what she said. He wrote it on a piece of paper, and it said, "See you later." I went to my last class and looked up the words in my Korean-English dictionary. "See" meant "to meet socially, especially often or regularly." I knew that "You" obviously meant "Me." My heart suddenly started beating faster and faster, and my face began burning red without reason. I did not have to know the rest of the words, but finally, I looked up the word "Later."

Even if I paid my undivided attention to American History, I would not have known whether the teacher was talking about the discovery of America or the invention of the first metal ship in the world. The only thing I could think of was, "She wants to meet me later!" Forty-five minutes seemed like an eternity and as soon as the last bell rang, I took off running to the library and waited for her. I missed my bus and waited until the librarian turned off the light and locked the library door. She pointed at her watch and said something to me, but my mind was too busy thinking about the girl.

It was a very long walk home, and somehow, I was not angry at her for not showing up. I was so worried about her that I secretly prayed that nothing bad happened to her and to let me see her tomorrow. The next day, she showed up at the same time, and I was surprised to see her acting like nothing happened. Then, she said, "See you later," again as the bell rang. I thought, "She must have forgotten about our date yesterday. She will come this time." I waited for her in front of the library again. My bus was already gone, and the librarian turned off the light and locked the door. She spoke loudly and very slowly, "R- YOU-WAIT-TING-FOR-SOME-ONE?" If I knew how to say it in English, I would have screamed at her that I might not speak good English, but I was not a deaf. I was so mad at the girl and could not believe she did not keep her promise. After I got home, I went straight to my room and slammed the door. My sister knew something was wrong since she never saw me act this way before, and she wanted to know why I missed the bus two days in a row.

She asked me what happened in school, and I told her that a girl who came to see me playing soccer wanted to meet me after school, but she did not show up for two days. I was furious and said things that did not make sense to her. She calmed me down and asked, "What were the exact words she said to you?" I proudly pulled out a sheet of paper from my back pocket and showed it to her. As soon as she saw "See you later" she fell to the floor laughing. I thought she went mad. She finally got up and said, "It meant good bye, Dummy!" I exclaimed, "Why can't she simply say bye?" The girl had no idea what I went through for the past two days. I was too embarrassed to see her again, because I could not believe how stupid I was. I thought that everybody was talking about me and laughing at me since my secret love for her was revealed; so I began to avoid her and my fourth period break after that!

The truth was that she did not come to see me play soccer or to talk to me at breaks, after all. Her boyfriend was a member of our team, and she only came to see him. I interpreted her friendliness completely wrong due to my lack of understanding of the American culture. You have to understand that Confucianism has a great influence on Korean customs and are embedded in social and family life. It emphasizes personal virtue and devotion to family. Thus, in order to keep a network of mutual duties binding families and social classes, Koreans are taught not only to respect elders and pay tributes to the spirit of their ancestors, but also to raise boys and girls in separate environments from an early age. From fourth grade until college, boys and girls attend schools segregated by sex, and of course, dating was only something to fantasize in dreams; the special one-on-one relationship and bonding between a boy and a girl did not exist in high school in Korea as it does in America.

While I was chasing a girl I was not allowed to love, there was another girl who loved me dearly, but secretly. I only knew her existence when she was around and failed to accept her love for me. After I married my wife and became accustomed to American life several years later, I realized that I totally did not see love when she was with me.

I found it not only intimidating, but tortuous being the only non-speaking student and being questioned by strangers about where I came from on the bus. I repeatedly said "Me no speaking English" to stop them from harassing me. However, it only encouraged them to speak to me more, and I was laughed at. Looking back, they, most of the time, were genuinely curious about me and no harm was intended. My sister had an irregular work schedule and would pick me up from school whenever she got off early from her work. I would wait for her in front of the double-door entrance. If she did not come by the time my bus left school, I would run to the back of the building and catch the bus at the last minute.

Next to the front asphalt parking lot, the marching band practiced on a grass field two to three times a week. I enjoyed watching them dance to the music that I had never heard before, while I was waiting for my sister to pick me up. The conductor was a girl, and she was adored by her peers and teachers because she was a leader of the student body government, nice to people, and already awarded a college scholarship. One afternoon, she parked her red firebird-Trans Am in front of me and asked me to ride with her. I did not have anything to say to a stranger, especially to a girl. Somehow, there was something about her that made me at ease and comfortable even though we did not have much to say. She pointed out the music playing on radio and simply said "You like?" I said, "Cha I cough ski (Tchaikovsky)." I do not know whether we had the same taste of music or she went to the store to buy what I liked. She always played my favorite songs the next day from Tchaikovsky's 1812 Overture to Pink Floyd's Wish You Were Here to Kansas's Dust in the Wind. On most days we did not have to speak a word while she was taking me home. However, it seemed like we spoke endlessly and felt I had known her for a long time. I was saddened to see my driveway too soon, for I had a wonderful time just being with her.

To overcome the uncomfortable silence during rides home with her and to show her my English skills, I memorized certain words and practiced with her. When she wore a hat one day I told her, "No hat. You obsolete!" She showed me her index finger and said, "One more time." Pointing at her hat I said, "You obsolete. No hat!" The night before I had looked up in my dictionary and found the word that I wanted to say. What I wanted to say was for her not to wear her hat because it made her look old. At first, I thought about what I wanted to say in Korean; then, found the English words that fit. In my dictionary, obsolete meant old.

Right after the see-you-later incident, she came to my sister's house and asked my sister if she could take me to prom. I did not know anything about prom and had never owned a tuxedo or suit in my life because all Korean students wore uniforms. My sister tried to explain to me about prom and how important it was to high school seniors, especially to girls. I had absolutely no idea about prom and dating. Since I was still so mad at the girl who had said "see you later" and never meant what she said, I refused, "No, I do not want to go to prom with her!" Later I learned that many boys asked her to be their date, but she turned them all down and simply did not go to prom. She had already bought her prom dress and offered my sister to buy me a tuxedo after she found out I did not have one. Knowing how nice she was and how much she enjoyed being with me, my sister desperately tried to convince me and even threatened me to change my mind, but I was so heart broken by another girl that I did not think about this one, and I broke her heart. How foolish I was! She did not express her sadness to me and continued driving me home after school after prom. After graduation she left me without saying good-bye and moved to Kentucky to attend the University of Kentucky.

As I witnessed my daughter's prom, I realized what I did to the girl was unforgiving, even if it was not my intention to hurt her feelings, and I simply did not know better. She might have already forgiven me, or I might be her forgotten boy, but I just can't forgive myself and forget what I did to her. Our club sponsors long term youth exchange student programs every year. My wife and I have had privileges of hosting students from all different countries. I truly enjoyed sharing our lives with them, and I terribly missed them when they went back to their homes. My Lowenstein is gone, and she only lives in my memory now. All youth exchange students remind me of my high school years and especially my Lowenstein.

Their heart will be broken by someone, and they will break somebody else's heart. Spring is not far behind to those who endured the cold winter. I'd like to have my youth exchange students experience more pains than pleasures, endure hardships than seek easiness, and love blindly than count failure before they even try. Lowenstein left us and broke our heart. I truly want our youth exchange students to have the best time of their life while they are with us; I want to be there to hug them and encourage them when they are down and do not want to get up to face obstacles. At last, I will tell them that they have to be Lowenstein for somebody like my Lowenstein in my heart did to me.

ShelterBox

"Why should I pick you as a SRT?" SRT (Shelterbox Response Team) Coordinator Jim Miller asked me in a hotel room in Atlanta, putting a stack of applications on the table to conclude the interview. The last question was hovering over my head. At this critical moment, I was thinking about the wonderful time I had with youth exchange students in Memphis the day before. I watched Jim and US Program Director, David Eby, impatiently awaiting my answer, "Yes, Kim is the one we are looking for."

I, on the other hand, could not convince myself why I was there in the first place. In the beginning I thought there had to be something I could contribute to ShelterBox organization. After listening to selections and screening procedures for SRT candidates, I realized my passion alone could not perform what SRTs were asked to help people displaced by disaster. I simply had none of the required qualifications to be safe, represent ShelterBox, and get a job done.

On January 12, 2008, I took several foreign youth exchange students living in the Nashville area to Memphis for a monthly activity that our district offers to all inbound and outbound students. I met with Tommy Martin's team from Clifton and Glen Vanderford's team from Jackson, and the twenty of us headed to Memphis on a chilly Saturday morning. We toured Elvis Presley's Graceland, listened to Blues at Beales Street, and ate famous hamburgers at Huey's, where the youngsters could easily blow toothpicks through drinking straws and stick them to the ceiling; no adult Rotarians could imitate the simple task. Then we saw the ducks in the lobby's fountain escorted to the elevator on the red carpet at Peabody Hotel. We visited the rundown hotel where Martin Luther King, Jr. was assassinated. One evening we rode a trolley looping downtown, and PDG Glen pointed out the stone where slaves were traded and sold to cotton plantation owners only a few hundred years ago. Overlooking the mighty Mississippi River, the stone quietly stood, unchained.

The next morning, I drove four and a half hours for the interview in Atlanta and wasn't quite convinced why I had even applied to be a SRT. Jim and David appeared to have made their decisions before listening to my last answer; somehow, I felt my answer would make no impact on them whatsoever. I delivered my last words with relief. "You asked me, 'why should ShelterBox pick me as a SRT?' At first, on my way here, I thought there had to be something I could contribute to ShelterBox." I quietly continued to speak from my heart, "Now, I have realized I am not only physically fit to carry what I am asked to do, but I also have no basic qualifications to finish a job. But I tell you this; if you do not pick me, I will be missed. If you do, I will make you proud." Then, I drove back to Hendersonville. A week later I received an email from Jim confirming they had made a right decision; they picked the twelve best candidates out of all applications for a weekend training in Florida, and I wasn't invited.

A year earlier, I learned about ShelterBox in Rotarian magazine, and PDG Glen Vanderford and David Eby set up the tent and gave several presentations in district conferences. The uniqueness of ShelterBox concepts and effectiveness of volunteers through Rotary clubs in the world interested me a great deal; however, it did not inspire me to take action. Then, in October, 2007, the moment for me to get involved finally came when I saw a little North Korean girl standing in front of her family's tent provided by ShelterBox right after the massive flooding. That was a very personal matter to me since my dad was born and raised in North Korea before the communists invaded that region.

He was the youngest of twelve brothers and sisters. When the Korean War broke out on the 25th of May, 1950, his entire family of twelve scattered. Somehow in the midst of chaos, he was able to escape death by a miracle and joined the South Korean army and fought against communists. In the South Korean army he miraculously united with two of his older brothers, and for the rest of his life, he did not have the opportunity to contact nor unite with the rest of his family in North Korea again. It drove him insane not knowing whether they survived or were killed during the Korean War, and he had to live with that pain until he died.

When my dad died in July 23, 2007, his last wish was to see his homeland for the last time. He was one of millions of Koreans who were separated since 1950 and never got to see his family again for almost 60 years. After the fall of the Berlin Wall, Korea remains the only divided country in the world. While South Korea's economy ranks the 8th highest in the world, communist North Korea is completely cut off from the rest of the world, and North Koreans still live behind the Iron Curtain. Over the years non governmental organizations offered to help North Koreans when they had ongoing famine and disasters. However, North Korea rarely opened the border to accept humanitarian aid until ShelterBox. I learned that torrential rain and an overflowing dam destroyed one-third of the country's crops. The worst was hundreds of people died, and thousands were displaced by flood. ShelterBox was the only organization allowed to enter the demilitarized zone to deliver 200 boxes. Seeing it with my naked eyes, I was completely sold to ShelterBox. I wanted to fulfill my dad's last wish by becoming a

SRT, visiting his homeland, helping North Koreans when another disaster occurs. I pray it will never happen, but we all know that disaster can occur anytime and anywhere. Ironically, North Korea made the strongest statement to the world about ShelterBox organization after receiving boxes from ShelterBox. Even North Korea acknowledged that ShelterBox received no funds from any governments and had no affiliations with political and religious organizations.

Then, what are ShelterBox and Shelterbox Response Team (SRT)? All SRTs represent Rotary based ShelterBox organization (www.shelterbox.org) which is a first response disaster relief operation based in England. Founder and CEO Tom Henderson is an ex-UK Royal Navy Search and Rescue diver and has been a member of Helston-Lizard Rotary club for over 20 years. He watched the news one evening, and there showed a disaster. Most of us watched, witnessed, and even personally knew vulnerable people displaced by disasters such as Tsunami, Katrina, and the Earthquake in China. Most people become numb to these kinds of news since it happens all the time. We think the disaster is too enormous for one person to do something about it. Tom spent days pondering on what he should do and how he could help. He came up with a list of things he would need for survival if his family were faced with disaster. He developed the idea of the "ShelterBox," and it became the millennium project for his Rotary Club in 2000.

ShelterBox is a global Rotary Club project that provides humanitarian aid in the form of shelter, warmth, comfort, and dignity to people displaced by natural and manmade disaster. As of May, 2009, ShelterBox sent aid to over 50 countries, had 85 deployments, and provided shelter to more than 800,000 of the most needed people. It is the biggest Rotary Club project in the history of Rotary International.

The box weighs about 130 pounds and contains essential needs for survival from six months to a year: a 10 person tent, thermal blankets, insulated ground sheets, mosquito nets, a water purification system, a water container, cooking equipment (a multi-fuel stove, cooking pans, pots, and utensils), a basic tool kit (hammer, axes, saw, trenching shovel, ropes) and school supplies.

The first shelterboxes were sent to Gujarat in India in January 2001. In the beginning, a handful of dedicated and trained volunteers in England were able to provide shelters to people displaced by disaster. However, the Tsunami in the spring of 2005 completely changed the operation of ShelterBox organization. By default, ShelterBox became a major player in providing first response disaster relief to people displaced by disaster.

However, I learned of the selection procedure and history of US SRT during the interview. The first US SRTs were recruited, trained, and deployed in 2007. After careful screenings of applications, those who have the required qualifications and commit long-term to the SRT program are invited to the interview. Those candidates are primarily working as police, paramedics, and firefighters so called "blue light." David Eby states, "SRT's are volunteers from around the world who give their time and energy to go into these environments and provide people the ability to survive the critical first days and weeks after a disaster." Because of these unique characteristics, ShelterBox carefully select the right individuals and train them to carry this important role. Then twelve candidates are selected from the interview and sent to Blackwater State Forest in Florida for a weekend of field training. Six out of twelve candidates are selected and invited to international training in Helston, Cornwall, England. They have to compete with candidates from other countries who went through the same procedure in their countries and must complete the entire program and be passed by ShelterBox trainers in order to be a SRT.

My will and my passion alone were not enough to be a Shelterbox Response Team member, no matter how hard I tried and how committed I was; however, ShelterBox called me late August, 2008, and I was 1 of the 12 invitees to the weekend training in North America; invitees were from all walk of life from Vancouver Island, Canada to Miami, Florida. ShelterBox must have seen something in me that I did not even know I had. After all, I was 1 of the 4 chosen to go to England for the final 9 day training: I from Hendersonville, Tennessee, Steven Tonkinson from Miami, Florida, Yi Shun Lai from Chicago, Illinois, and John Cordell from Vancouver, Washington. The 4 of us representing USA joined with 12 other candidates from other countries, and we were told it was the first time in ShelterBox history that all candidates completed the course and became SRTs at the same time. All we got from ShelterBox was a green t-shirt for successfully finishing the course. It was worth going through this intense, military like training to be a special, unique team called SRT. In 2009, there are only 32 SRTs in North America and 130 in the world.

Tom Henderson and trainers in England said during the last briefing with each candidate, "Kim, you did not have the skills to do the job when you arrived, and we weren't sure if you were going to make it because you seemed lost the moment you got here." He jokingly said, "No one understands your Southern English here in England, but we can see you'd rather die while trying to help the most needed people in disaster." If that was the only reason why I was selected as a SRT, what an honor it was, and let me not lose my will and my passion for why I wanted to be a SRT at the first place, and let me die with an unchanged heart.

I came back to the States in March 2, 2009 from the training in England. The current Rotary International President was to visit our club the following month. I told committee members, President Elect Robin Williams, Secretary Buddy Shaw, and Past President Eddie Roberson that I might have to deploy within 48 hours if I get a call from the ShelterBox head quarter in England. We had to prepare for my not being here when R.I. President would visit our club. Of course, I wanted to be there for R.I. President D.K. Lee and his wife Jung, and R.I. Trustee John Germ and his wife Judy. At the same time, I had no doubt Robin and her committee would do a great job whether I were here to preside the meeting or not. I truly believed R.I. President, D.K. Lee would not only understand my absence when he visited but also support my decision in helping disaster victims whole heartedly. Thankfully he came, and I had the privilege of travelling to Cookeville, Tennessee, with him and met Past R.I. President Jim Lacy and Father of Polio Plus movement Bill Sergeant. What great Rotarians they are!

On my 47th birthday, I received an email asking if I was willing to deploy to Brazil with Wayne Robinson an SRT from Atlanta. When SRTs are called to deploy we have to be deployed within 48 hours. I immediately thanked Head Quarters for selecting me for the job. Brazil had a major flood in the northeast region. Six cities, the size of Alaska, were flooded on the evening of May 6, 2009. The following day, Associated Press estimated over 300,000 people were displaced by the flood and hundreds of people died within a day. I drove to Atlanta at 2 a.m. on Monday morning. Wayne and I were to visit the Brazilian Consulate first thing the next morning to get our visas. We quickly explained ShelterBox to them and why we needed our visas immediately so that we could fly out that afternoon to Brazil to help people devastated by flooding. We were shocked to hear that we not only could not get our visas that morning but were told we had to make an appointment a week later; then it would take another two to three months for us to get volunteer visas since we were going to help people, not as tourists! Rotary Clubs and the District Governor in Brazil were waiting for us to arrive since we had already established necessary contacts for them to help us on custom, translators, transportation, and other major issues. I stayed with Wayne in Atlanta for two days to resolve the visa situation with no avail. It was very frustrating that even North Korea opened the border for ShelterBox, but our friendly neighboring country Brazil refused to issue visas because of bureaucracy.

In the meantime, I met with Robin Williams and told her my situation since I would not be there for next week's club meeting and monthly board meeting. It was the same situation as Robin and I had to prepare for the R.I. President knowing I might not be there due to ShelterBox deployment. She understood and gave me full support; then, I emailed board members explaining why I could not attend our regular meeting and board meeting on the following week. I did not expect everyone to understand or give full support for what I chose to do. Even my own wife disapproved of my being a SRT member because of situations like this; her husband had to sacrifice his own and his family's daily life over disaster victims in foreign countries. She worried that her husband would be deployed to dangerous and unstable places for two to four weeks. In the end, she understood why I chose to be a SRT and acknowledged it as the right thing for her to support.

What surprised me most were several comments our club members and board members made verbally and in email after they knew I would be absent for several weeks, and that I might not even be there for our banquet, celebrating our 40th anniversary. They said that I should stay home to take care of my family and to preside weekly club meetings. Furthermore, they said that there would be many more disasters after I finished my term as president, and then I could go out to help people. I was accused of neglecting my duty as president and abandoning our club for a few weeks. I explained that it was to help disaster victims! I could not believe some members actually thought that presiding over club meetings were more important than saving the lives of flood victims in Brazil. Also, some members thought that no person other than the president could run the meetings.

If a leader of an organization thought that he was the only person that could run his organization and failed to develop and train next leaders, then the future of that organization is doomed, in my opinion. That was exactly what I want to leave behind when my term is over in June 2009. The next leader of our club is not only capable of running our club, but more importantly, Robin would take us to the next level. I truly believe in that because I invested so much time and effort in developing the next leaders. If there is a big hole to fill after I leave my presidency, it is not because of my leadership being too great to be filled; it is because I failed to train the next leader. That is the fact; no more or no less. It is wrong of me to compare my beliefs and my life to others without walking in their shoes. Each of us has a journey of our own, and it is the path I chose to live by "Service Above Self."

I responded to those members saying, "Talk is cheap to me. I would rather lead by example and die while serving others instead of waiting for a better time to help. That time will never come since I will always put it off, make excuses, and think it is not the right time. You are absolutely right and I should wait until my term is over." Members said to me, "You should stay here and finish out the rest of your term," and "There will be many trips with ShelterBox once your term is over." If I can help one child from polio right now, I do not want to wait another day. If I can help one child from dying from hunger today, I can't wait any longer; tomorrow is too late. If I hear crying for a helping hand, I want to give my hand when I am able to help. If I can help one victim from this flood that killed over 100 people in one day and displaced an estimate of over 300,000 people in two days, I can't wait for another day when the opportunity comes for me to help those people. My dear friend and fellow Rotarian Tom Andrews says, "If you can, you should." How long can we wait for the right time to help and how long will it go on? How many more have to die until I do something about it? If I failed to do my job as a president by volunteering to help people when I should be presiding meetings instead, so be it. This position has offered me many opportunities to help people in need and work with leaders in our community. Also, it allows me to meet many wonderful Rotarians in other Rotary Clubs, District, and International by working together for the good of Rotary. Most of all, it helps me to be a better person, and 4 Way Test is the true reminder how I should live daily. Therefore, if this position prevents me from doing what we are supposed to do, I should be removed from this position immediately. I realize I have been living the wrong life.

I was so furious and could not express such emotion in writing. I counted from one to ten and ten to fifty over and over to calm me down. The more I counted, the more I could not help but think of the numbers of people I could save. As a matter of fact, there are only 32 SRTs—first response team members trained in North America to help disaster victims. I was trained to help people devastated by disaster and there was no way in the world I could turn my back on those people in need of my help and ignore my calling.

Wayne and I did not get our visas and had to ask SRTs from the UK to go to help for us after all. On my way home from the Brazilian Consulate, I confronted God on why He did not want me to go. Did He not want me to help those victims? Since I was back in town, I went to our regular club meeting, and I had to ask all club members what they wanted me to do; should I stay here to run the meetings or deploy to help disaster victims? They looked at me with curious eyes asking why I asked such an obvious question. They all said, "You should go," and at least, the majority of our members knew what was more important. The same week, I got my answer from God about why He wanted me here next to S.T.

The next day I would be heading to Atlanta to get my visa and I wanted to have a last meal with S.T. before I left the country. S.T. had been battling with cancer and could not eat much due to radiation and chemo treatment. S.T. and I had breakfast at Cracker Barrel on Saturday morning and I left for Atlanta the following day. Since I was back in town without a visa, he and I were to go to the District Conference together the following Friday and Saturday. I called him early in the morning on Saturday, but he did not answer. On Monday, I found out that S.T was admitted to the hospital. I rushed to the CCU and Mary Ann told me he fell late Saturday night and he was too weak to see people. I visited him for next two days and talked with Mary Ann and their daughter Sandy and their granddaughter. I left the hospital around 4:45 pm on Tuesday with a fellow Rotarian, Don Claussen, and it was 7:45 pm when Mary Ann called me at home saying S.T. died around 7 p.m. I clearly heard what she said the first time, but I asked her again and again what she said to me. I broke down on the floor and cried. I should have been strong for Mary Ann on the other line but S.T. was like my dad, and he treated me as I was his son. I begged Mary Ann to see him and rushed to the hospital, where

I met fellow Rotarians, Robin Williams, Bill Taylor, and Brenda Payne. The four of us hugged each other in the parking lot and cried. When we went to the CCU unit to see S.T., he was already moved to a funeral home. Brenda and Robin said, "This is why you could not go to Brazil. S.T. wanted you to be here for him."

The next day, Mary Ann asked me to come to the funeral home, where I met her and their three daughters, Sandy, Jeannie, and Becky. Sandy took me to a room where S.T. laid and said, "My dad always thought of you as his son and you are a family member. You are the only person seeing him." I was more than thankful for me and my wife to see him and say how much I loved him; I promised I would carry on his Rotary legacy, and the role of S.T. and be as influential as he was to me. The man who invited me to the club died during my presidency. I remembered how proud he was at the reception, talking and taking pictures with first Korean R.I. President D.K. Lee and me.

I asked God, "What is life?" He answered, "You are a mist that appears for a little while and then vanishes….Life is like the grass that will soon wither, like green plants they will die away." Life is like a cloud in the sky, not knowing where to come and where to go. I came naked from my mother's womb and will be departed naked at death. I should put in a splendid performance on stage while I am alive. Life is so precious and every human being has a life worth living; each of us is placed in this world with specific reason. Our paths are directed by God, and it is our duty to live, love, and leave our legacy until He calls us home. God continues to say, "Anyone, then, who knows the good he ought to do and does not do it, sins." Confucius says, "To know what is right and not do it is the worst cowardice." It is not important whether we are from the east or west, and it does not matter what kinds of background we have. There is a time we have to decide. Socrates said, "The unexamined life is not worth living." Most only exist and not really live. I do not know what is going to happen tomorrow. Let me live the best I can, enjoy every moment I have today, and thank God for what I have and what He has in heaven for us.

"…the things that began to happen after that were so great and beautiful that I cannot write them. And for us this is the end of all the stories, and we can most truly say that they all lived happily ever after. But for them it was only the beginning of the real story. All their life in this world and all their adventures had only been the cover and title page: now at last they were beginning Chapter One of the Great Story which no one on earth has read: which goes on forever: in which every chapter is better than the one before." C.S. Lewis

The End of the Year Report Card

Tell me, is this the end of my journey as president of Hendersonville Rotary Club? When I became president in July 2008, we all knew my term would end in June this year. However, it came too suddenly. I find myself surprised, saddened, and empty at the same time. I am surprised to see so much unfinished business that the next president has to carry on. I could have done a better job if I knew then what I know now. Most of all, I feel empty because I did not accomplish my goal, 100% Paul Harris Fellow Club.

During the new member induction ceremony, I tell them that our club strives to be the best in the following areas. First goal is to increase our membership by 10%. We started with 149 members, and we brought 27 new members in this year. Our second goal is to implement a successful project that addresses the need of our community and communities in other countries. Joe Beaver and Kent Cochran implemented the Dictionary Project which made sure that all 2,300 third graders in Sumner County received a dictionary. Also, our Guatemala Project of dental, medical, or vision was very successful; the goal was to serve 1,000 patients according to Rip and Bill. We actually saved 1,441 Guatemalan lives—almost doubling previous trips to that country. The third is to support the Rotary Foundation through both program participation and financial contribution—we have 43 new Paul Harris Fellows and 45 Sustaining Members this year! I became a SRT (ShelterBox Response Team) member to help people displaced by disaster, and our club donated to ShelterBox for an international project.

The four is to develop leaders capable of serving in Rotary beyond the club level. I believe we approved when current Rotary International President and his wife, and RI Trustee John Germ and his wife Judy, visited our club in April 2009? Also our club leaders attended all district seminars and learned about our District and Rotary International. They came back anew and expressed how much they learned and were amazed by all the programs that Rotary International and the Rotary Foundation offers to people all over the world. The more we learn, we can't help but love Rotary and have deep appreciation for the mission of Rotary.

I have been sending thank you cards to all members in our club because of my sincere appreciation for their support and dedication to Rotary. I admit it has not been easy to send thank you cards to RNOs. Do you remember RNOs (Rotarians Name Only?) My effort seems useless, and it seems impossible to shift members to true Rotarians; however, I want to do my part anyway. Someone once said, "Today's impossibilities are tomorrow's miracles." My belief that I can make a difference will create the reality in this world.

Therefore, I believe that the biggest mistake in life is doing nothing, and waiting for the right moment to act even if I can only do a little, I try my best. I spent my whole life building my dream from nothing. Yet, one disaster can destroy that dream. I build it anyway.

One car accident can end my dream of walking down the aisle holding my daughter's hand in her wedding. I dream it anyway.

My dream of being a GSE (Group Study Exchange) team leader to other countries can be shattered because a team leader to Nigeria was kidnapped and nowhere to be found. I want to lead young professionals to Turkey next year anyway.

It is rewarding to help people displaced by disaster; at the same time, I put myself in a dangerous situation. I want to deploy to disaster countries and help them anyway.

The goodness and kindness that I have shown this morning will be forgotten before the nightfall. Do good and be kind anyway.

The trees I have planted may be cut down and burnt. It will take another life time to see the fruits of the trees, but I want to plant the trees anyway. Even if the world were to end tomorrow, I will plant the seed for tomorrow anyway.

I live by the Rotary motto, "Service Above Self," and 4 Way Test. People make fun of me and laugh at our mission. I live by "Service Above Self" anyway.

It seems to be a useless act sometimes, but I want to do it anyway because that is why I became a Rotarian.

Two years ago, at the Christmas for Kids event, I rode Martina McBride's bus to pick four elementary students in Portland. I left Hendersonville at ten in the morning to pick them up and went back to their school at 9:30 at night to drop them off. Parents of one of the kids were not there, and the bus driver and I had to wait for kid's parents. When his father finally showed up, he was drunk and did not care for his daughter's joy or Christmas gifts for her family. I was pondering on why I even volunteered to do this. I thought, "See, nobody cares." Then on my way home, Martina McBride's song, 'Do it Anyway" was playing over the radio.

"You can spend your whole life building something from nothing. One storm can come and blow it all away.
Build it anyway.
You can chase a dream that seems so out of reach.
And you know it might not ever come your way.

Dream it anyway."

The second reason why I sent a personal thank you cards to all of our club members at the end of the year was to ask them to continue to support President Robin through this coming year. Her goal is to have 100% participation from all club members.

We have been very successful on some events, such as the Festival by the Lake and Days of Wine and Roses, which over 70 to 80 % of members participated on both sponsorship or volunteering. At the same time, we have been very disappointed at the lack of participation on programs like Roadside Clean up, Wheels in Motions, and District activities.

20 % of Rotarians doing 80 % of the work may be normal, but it is not acceptable to our club. Historically, less than 5 to 10 % of members supported Roadside Clean Up, and some members complained for the lack of fellowship opportunities and networking. Let me tell you this: while picking up trash for Roadside Clean Up, waiting to give away bikes to students for Wheels in Motions, pouring wine at the Days of Wine and Roses, flipping hamburgers at the Festival by the Lake, and riding together to District Assembly, I experienced the best fellowship and got to know them personally, and it was more than enough.

I admit the majority of organizations, including Rotary clubs, throughout the world fall in this category- 20/80 principle. 20 to 80 % of participation is good according to standard. But as members of the Hendersonville Rotary Club, that is not acceptable. 100% participation is expected from the day a new member joins our club. I said on the program of 40th Annual the Rotary Club of Hendersonville Awards and Installation Banquet on June 19, 2009:

"I believe the person I see this moment and whom I am thinking of is the most important person. I believe the most important time is right now, the most important work is what I am doing now, and the most important way, as a Rotarian, is to live by the Rotary motto, "Service Above Self," until my time on this earth ends. Thank you for giving me an opportunity to do what I am passionate about."

Not all of you will get to read my personal thank you notes to each and every member in this book. To tell you the truth, it was difficult for me to be honest and say what I was thankful for when it came down to members who are RNO. I did not even know some members at all, despite he or she being one of our own club members! However, there is something genuinely nice about each member, and I have realized every member can be a true Rotarian and can serve.

Thank you for allowing me to serve you, and thank you for the unforgettable memories as a member of the Hendersonville Rotary Club.

"The Paradoxical Commandments"

Give the world the best you have, and you'll get kicked in the teeth.

Give the world the best you have anyway.

Honesty and frankness make you vulnerable.

Be honest and frank anyway. (By Dr. Kent M. Keith)

PART TWO

LETTERS TO PRESIDENTS-ELECT

August Letter

Seventeen months ago, on January 14, 2012, I was nominated to be a District Governor for 2014-2015. I have ardently prepared myself to the best of my knowledge, to be the best governor I can be. I hope you are inspired, motivated, and equipped to lead your own club to the best of your ability. Also I hope to make our district one of best Rotary districts in the world.

I found a quote that gives me a reason to get up each morning, and a purpose driven life to fulfill my goals before I finally become a District Governor next year. They are the inspiring words of Paul "Bear" Bryant, who has said, "It's not the will to win that matters. Everyone has that. It's the will to prepare to win that matters." I believe that your success as President of your club on July 1, 2014 will depend on the will to prepare yourselves right now as President-Elect. I am 100% sure that you want to make a difference and to do projects that leave a lasting legacy for generations to come. Otherwise, you would not be chosen to serve as President of your Rotary Club, whether you willingly accept your duty or not. You and I have many months to prepare; however, if I fail to prepare, that means I have failed you. If you fail to prepare, you fail not only your club but also your community and the lives of others that depend on you. Whether we succeed or fail, it is up to me as District Governor Elect and you as President-Elect.

When I was President-Elect of the Hendersonville Rotary Club in 2007, I started writing monthly letters to my club members. I mailed them to their homes so their whole families could share my personal story and learn about the Rotary. My club had 145 members, but I admit that not all 145 members were Rotarians, let alone that I was not even sure myself if I were passionate enough about Rotary and whether I had what it takes to be a leader in my heart. Ever since I joined Rotary club and went on a few mission trips with fellow Rotarians to impoverished countries, I learned to believe that Rotary is Service Above Self. I believe that without building a personal relationship with my fellow Rotarians that was based on trust, honesty, and integrity, not only would I not be an effective leader but no one would follow in my steps.

As soon as I became a club President, I stopped sending them my letters. I have not stopped writing. While I was writing to the unknown everyday for six years, I pondered over why I agonized over a self-inflicted wound, revealing my naked vulnerability to the public. Now I know why I have been writing letters that are not to be sent until 2008. I did not know then that I would serve as a District Governor one day, but I know now that I was writing to you.

Abraham Lincoln once said, "If I had eight hours to chop down a tree, I'd spend six sharpening my axe." You and I have one opportunity to do something great. While we are given time to learn, plan, and prepare, let us do everything we can do to prepare ourselves to meet our challenges, and to show the world what we have prepared for. When the moment comes for us to lead in July next year, it will be the greatest moment of all. Of course, we may be mocked and laughed at, some might even think it is an impossible dream. Let's dare to dream. Let's do something big that never has been done before. I hope you would look forward to receiving the next month's letter. I will unveil our dream in the letter of September. Thank you so much, and I cannot wait to work with you.

***

Dear Presidents and Assistant Governors,

Receiving a copy of my letter to President-Elects, you will find why I am writing a letter to all of sixty-two club President-Elects each month. Nevertheless, you may be wondering why I have sent you the same letter as well. For Assistant Governors, I feel that you should not only know what is being communicated between District Governor-elect and President-Elects for their year in 2014-2015, but should also be actively engaged in planning and encouraging future leaders.

Since your club has not yet selected your President-Elect, I'd like to send you my monthly letter and hope you would forward my letters to your President-Elect as soon as he or she is selected. I believe it is one of my responsibilities as District Governor-Elect to give all President-Elects an equal opportunity to succeed even though one is not selected yet.

Thank you in advance for your understanding, and I hope you select your President-Elect soon so that I can directly communicate with that Rotarian.

President-Elect Training Schedules

Dear President-Elect *(or President if your PE is as yet un-named)*,

Within a few days, you will be receiving the September letter from me. But before that, I'd like to lay out training schedules specifically designed for you to be prepared before you take office in July 2014. About this time last year, I was in Huntsville, Alabama, attending five day training as DGN (District Governor Designate). It seems like just yesterday, but today I am preparing myself for GETS (Governor Elect Training Seminar) in Lexington, Kentucky from September 17th thru 22nd. When Rotarians accept the position of District Governor-elect or President-elect, they are expected to attend trainings, and Rotary International even mandates for all DGE to attend Rotary International Assembly in San Diego in January 2014 (Rotary brings all 535 District Governor-elects from all over the world.)

And all President-elects of 34,000 Rotary clubs in the world must attend PETS (President Elect Training Seminar) in their countries. If they do not attend, they do not get to serve. It shows how important it is to develop and train leaders in order for them to be successful. In addition, our district asks the President-elect to attend the following trainings to be the best leaders they can be: 1. The Rotary Leadership Institute. 2. Pre-PETS 3. President Elect Training Seminar. 4. District Assembly.

1. The Rotary Leadership Institute (Parts I, II & III) is scheduled for multiple locations/dates.
Oct 5, 2013 at the Jackson Chamber from 8:15 to 3 pm.
Nov 16, 2013 at the Renaissance Center in Dickson from 8:15 to 3 pm.
Feb 1, 2014 at the Doubletree Hotel in Murfreesboro from 8:15 to 3 pm.

Registration is now open for Saturday, October 5 in Jackson; Saturday, November 16 in Dickson and Saturday, February 1, 2014 in Murfreesboro. Please visit our district website or http://www.hoa-rli.com/ to register.

The courses are designed to provide Rotary knowledge and to develop leadership skills for voluntary organizations. RLI is fun, interactive, participatory, and uses top faculty and facilitation techniques to make the experience valuable and enjoyable.
 If you have not previously taken an RLI course, you will need to register for Part I. You can only take one part per day since all three parts are full day sessions. You must have completed Part I to take Part II and must have completed Parts I & II to take Part III.

This all day training provides a notebook (Part I), a light Continental Breakfast and Lunch, plus access to other up and coming Rotary club leaders in the area. The Registration Fee is $70 per person ($85 if registration is received after 14 days preceding the event) and it is recommended that the clubs pay the registration fee. Please note that the RLI cancellation policy is for two weeks prior to the date the course is being conducted. You can register on-line at http://www.hoa-rli.com/ . For additional information, please contact Ed Maupin @ 615-867-3273 or via e-mail at maupinedward@bellsouth.net .

2. Pre-PETS (President Elect Training Seminar) October 26th, following Grant Management Seminar in Jackson, TN. Note that Pre-PETS will immediately follow the Grant Management Seminar and will last approximately 90 minutes. All PEs should attend both the Seminar and Pre-PETS in order for their clubs to be certified, learn how to apply for Grants, and to attend Pre-PETS.

3. PETS (President Elect Training Seminar) from March 21 thru 23, 2014. It is mandated from Rotary International that all PE must attend. Otherwise, President-elect does not get to serve as President.

4. District Assembly in April is often called Club Leadership Training. Club president-elect builds on PETS training to gain leadership skills, while other incoming club leaders learn their new responsibilities. Club leadership teams refine their goals for the year.

Please put those important training dates on your calendars and learn as much as possible in order for you to do the best job possible. I am doing the same thing as DGE. I surely do not want to fail you, our district, and the communities we serve. I am looking forward to seeing all of you at RLI, Pre-PETS, PETS, and District Assembly. First things first, please register for RLI Part I, II, or III on Oct 5 in Jackson today.

Thank you.

Truly Yours in Rotary,
DGE Kim Kim

September Letter

"It always seems impossible until it's done."—Nelson Mandela

    I have known many of you and have visited almost all of the clubs in our district several times in the past. I am always grateful when I am asked to share my personal stories with your club members: stories about saving the lives of disaster victims in the rubble of the earthquake in Haiti as a ShelterBox Response Team member, giving polio vaccines to hundreds of children in Africa, installing electricity in remote villages in Honduras to transform lives forever, going on dental, vision, medical mission trips to Guatemala with my fellow Rotarians, and many more life changing experiences I have had since I became a Rotarian. Yet I admit that this does not give me any right to send you my letters each month. I have no way of knowing how you interpret my passion and my purpose of writing letters to you, and I can only apologize if I have ever offended you. I am truly sorry for that and am willing to accept any harsh words. At the same time, I will not rest until my dream comes true, no matter how long it takes or how difficult it is for every Rotary club in our district to be a 100% Paul Harris Club!

    Looking back, it seems like it could have only been a dream for a seventeen year old Korean boy to come to America and later become a District Governor of Rotary, the finest service organization in the world. I have been given the gift of an opportunity to make a difference. Whether we accept the challenge in front of us or run from it, it is no coincidence that you and I have been given an once in a lifetime opportunity to end polio for good. It upsets me to my core when I think of the children I saw in Africa, crippled and treated inhumanely because they were paralyzed by polio.

They could not do the simple things many children take for granted: walking with two legs, or holding a spoon with one hand. However, their souls were not crippled. A child should never be destined to a life of pain and his dreams should not be shattered before they were even begun because of polio.

I truly believe every child deserves a chance to live and experience his own story to tell to the world. As I am writing this letter today on September 8, 2013, there is an article in the Sunday Tennessean titled, "Militants impede polio aid," mentioning an obstacle we faced in Pakistan, one of three endemic countries. Two parents, out of desperation, smuggled polio vaccines to save their three children from polio and lived in fear that the Islamic militants would find out, and that they would be killed just like dozens of vaccination workers and volunteers had.

Do you know what the worst part of all this is? There is something every Rotarian can do. Since Rotary declared to the world that we would eradicate polio from the face of the earth in 1985, it has become our moral obligation to finish what we started. Just sixty cents a vaccine eliminates a child from the risk of polio and gives him the ability to walk to school, to play with his friends at the playground, to hold hands with his parents, and to dream his dreams, however big or how small. We can help provide a child the simple pleasures in life, like his first steps, kicking a soccer ball for the very first time, and the independence and adventure of exploring the world around him on his very own two feet.

I remember holding a two-hour-old baby in my arms and dispensing two drops of polio vaccine into its tiny mouth in Africa. Never shall I forget the face of the baby's mother and her words as long as I will live, still lying in bed after giving birth, she said, "You came all the way here from America to save my baby?" I flew twenty-one hours to the other side of the world and spent thousands of my own money. It was because I promised my cousin who was crippled by polio when he was three years old in Korea that one day I would buy him a wheelchair, which I never did. I was seventeen years old when I made that promise and left him to come to America. I do not think my cousin remembered my promise, but I could never erase it out of my mind. The promise I made was constantly stationed in the back of my mind. For that reason, I was doing it for all the wrong reasons: so I could be free from the anguish and guilt. Until the moment she said that, I had not realized the depth of what I was doing and the effect it had on lives outside of my own. Though I may never cross paths with her or her child again, I helped impact that child's life. In that moment, I felt such joy for her baby, knowing the child in my arms would grow up and live a normal life, never experiencing polio like so many others have.

How can one ordinary man like me make a difference in the lives of others? Clem Renouf, Rotary International President of 1978-1979 said, "Rotary takes ordinary men and gives them extraordinary opportunities to do more with their lives than they ever dreamed possible." The truth is that if I alone dream of changing the world, I would probably give up before I even started because it would overwhelm me too much to even know where to begin. However, could I give polio vaccines to children? Yes, I could. Could I donate money for third graders to receive dictionaries? Yes, I could. Could I get up at four in the morning and take a youth exchange student with me to volunteer for Clarksville Sunrise Rotary Club's Bike Ride fundraising? Yes. I did that last Saturday, August 31. What fun we had working side by side with members from two Rotary clubs in Clarksville and Rotarian Tommy Martin from Clifton! These are such small random acts of kindness, yet I receive immeasurable satisfaction that money could not buy.

We cannot change the world completely. We cannot do everything. But to one child whom we may never know and who cannot afford even the basic necessities, we Rotarians can be the world to that child. Look at what we are doing on the polio campaign alone, out of thousands of projects Rotarians are doing at this very moment. It was started with one man's random act of kindness and because of Rotarians like him all over the world, polio will disappear from the world forever.

In my August letter to you, I said I would unveil my goal as District Governor for 2014-2015. In the beginning of this letter, I laid out what my goal is: 100% Paul Harris Fellow District. That means all 3,300 Rotarians in 62 clubs are asked to contribute to the Rotary Foundation 1,000 dollars during our year, starting when we take office in July. Some would say that this is an impossible dream. Some would argue that I cannot tell you what to do with your own money. Some might even say it is a crazy and laughable. The reality is, we might never reach our goal during our year. Then, you might ask, "Why do you set an impossible goal, setting club Presidents up to fail?" Well, the goal is not a matter of losing or winning, success or failure, nor am I making commands over what our members do with their finances. However, I am testifying that each and every step and donation towards our goal is a step closer to polio eradication.

Author of *Night* and Nobel Peace Prize winner Elie Wiesel writes, "I am not so naïve as to believe that this slim volume will change the course of history or shake the conscience of the world. Books no longer have the power they once had. Those who kept silent yesterday will remain silent tomorrow." I neither believe that I can inspire you to accomplish our goal merely with my words, nor do I believe that all 62 club presidents will follow suit. Unlike you, I am shamefully aware of my language barrier and limitation in words. You should know by now that my English is far from good. Because of these reasons, I am afraid to express my feelings in words—for it might convey the wrong messages. Why did I choose to write to you then? It is because I believe you and me, along with 62 club presidents, might not be given another chance to do what we are destined to do. It is no accident that the year of 2014, our district is celebrating our 100 year anniversary. Nashville Rotary Club is currently the 8th largest club in the world. When it was chartered in 1914, they were the first club in Tennessee, and thirteen members planted a seed to grow to 62 clubs and 3,300 members today.

If you ask me, "What is one thing you want to accomplish as a District Governor?" The answer would be to make our club a 100% Paul Harris Club. I truly believe it is our calling that you and I have been chosen to serve for the 100 year anniversary of our district. I have only one life to live and have been given a once- in-a- lifetime opportunity, so I refuse to be an idle spectator of my own life. There is an old saying that the best time to plant a tree is twenty years ago. The next best time is right now. Won't you join with me to plant a seed of 100% Paul Harris District? When I imagine twenty years later that people will come and sit in the shade of the tree you and I had planted, it makes me happy. I think that will be our greatest legacy to leave behind, but it is up to us individually how much we try to give ourselves into these efforts. I conclude this letter by the words of Elie Wiesel: "Our lives no longer belong to us alone; they belong to all those who needs us desperately."

October Letter

I have been contemplating what to write for this month because I have come to the conclusion that no words need to be added to what I have already said. Somehow, I cannot help but feel that the more I say the more my intent diminishes from the truth. Ever since you have joined Rotary, you have learned to love Rotary for what it does and what it stands for. You believe in "Service Above Self," and you are passionate about making a difference through the network and fellowship in Rotary. All of us had different motives when we first joined Rotary, but we remain in the Rotarian family for one reason, which is Service Above Self. You are given a distinct opportunity in your lives to leave a legacy when you become president of your club. I sincerely thank you for your willingness to accept challenges, to lead your club to its full potential, and to make it your personal responsibility to do good in the world. I am deeply moved by your commitment and will be your biggest supporter.

Young physician Mae Jemison was the first female African American astronaut. She said, "It's your place in the world; it's your life. Go on and do all you can with it, and make it the life you want to live." After all, as you are making it the life you want to live, you are actually making it a better world and a better life for others. I do not know about you, but I have lived more than two-thirds of my life already. I could see the end of my journey closing on this earth; it is passing me by quickly everyday. The time on my hand is not only limited, urgent, and precious, but what I do with the remainder also becomes the utmost important matter to me and how I want to close the final chapter of my life before I depart.

Because I came to America when I was young, and the fact that I looked like a foreigner, along with a strong accent, I was treated differently and looked upon as an outsider. My membership had been denied countless times by other reputable organizations, but Rotary was the only service organization that accepted me for who I was with open arms. I am always grateful for that even though it took me a long time to be invited. Having said that, membership in Rotary is not only dear to my heart, but it became a personal matter. I have been a member of the Rotary club since 2000, but Rotary became my way of life, two years after I joined. Growing up in Seoul, Korea, I had witnessed respected leaders, so called "movers and shakers" in the community, gathered together, cleaning the bank of rivers, sweeping the streets with white masks on, and visiting orphanages to give them baths and to feed them because they were all mentally challenged children and some adults. I will never forget the picture in a newspaper of a young, attractive, and petite female Rotarian with a yellow Rotary vest on, feeding a bowl of seaweed soup to a childlike man on her knee. It was heartwarming and her face resonated to me as an angel. I was struck by their good deeds and hoped to be a Rotarian, one day when I grew up, for they were living examples of how I wanted to live my life.

Rotary has changed my life. More specifically, Rotarians have changed my life. Rotary International President Maurice Duperrey said in his address to the 1938 Rotary Convention, "Rotary is so simple that many people do not understand it, and some even misunderstand it. Rotary is not a philosophy…not an all-embracing world point of view which answers every question…and satisfies all the dictates of the heart and mind. Rotary is merely an association of business and professional men united in the ideal of service." People often ask me why I still remain as a Rotarian after all these years even though I have done basically everything I set out to do. My answer to them is quite simple, like Rotarian Maurice said, "I will forever be a humble Rotarian because it gives me a purpose each day, and I fill each day and empty heart with a meaningful life for me, my family, and any others my life may touch."

Ever since I became a Rotarian, my family, work, and friends have told me that I have become a better father, husband, son, boss, co-worker, and most of all a better person. I am truly thankful for the opportunity given to me so that I could do all those things I could not do otherwise. Sooner or later, I will not be able to do what I love to do, physically and mentally. Therefore, I truly believe that any person who believes in Service Above Self and abides by The Four-Way Test can be a Rotarian. A statistic indicates only 15% of us invite new members. They should be invited to the Rotary club, no matter what type of vocation they have had. Rotary founder Paul Harris had a variety of jobs throughout his life, from reporter, seaman, fruit picker, hotel clerk to a granite salesman, and was a lawyer as well! Can you imagine what our world is going to be alike if anyone and anywhere is a Rotarian in every vocation and in every household? I could not agree more with Past RI President Edd McLaughlin, who said, "Rotary is without reality until men translate it into their lives and the lives of others. In short, you and I are Rotary."

I have traveled many countries participating in numerous Rotary projects that change lives and transform communities. However, it was not my true intention to change the world, from the beginning. I only wanted to change myself and maybe lead my young children by example. My youngest son, Doun, left for South Korea two months ago to participate on the long term youth exchange program right after graduating from high school. He was a member of Interact club and attended a five-day RYLA camp while he was in high school. He is only seventeen years old. Later on in this letter, you will read his first email to district youth exchange officer Tommy Martin and a letter from my daughter responding to my letter after coming back from my Haiti ShelterBox deployment in 2009. I believe you will see how Rotary has given my young children the best possible environment to grow up and how it shapes their minds. This is what Rotary does to young people especially. Doun was too shy and too introverted to function even in daily life. Reading his email, I could sense he has matured so much already and seems like he is finding his place in this world.

He writes on September 28, 2013:

Hey there Tommy, I am so sorry for such a late response. School is fun, I have made very kind friends and it has helped me improve my speaking ability. I feel extremely lucky to have my first host family. They are experienced at hosting students and they trust me very much.

In school, they study English, Korean, Geography, Film, Social Studies, Math, History, Biology, Chemistry, Art, and much more. The schedule is different every day.

I've been in Korea for about a month and a half, and during that time I have been to 5 universities (Seoul University was the nicest and the number one school in Korea), to a temple, to the beach, the world's largest department store, Seoul, Dangjin to visit my mom's family during Korean Thanksgiving with permission. (Rotary gave us Korean traditional clothing called hanboks), to a theme park. I've done so many things and haven't had much time to stay home, but I do not want to waste the opportunity and stay home.

I will be sure to send pictures soon when I transfer them from my phone.

I hope you and the Rotarians are doing well and please thank them for giving me the opportunity to travel here.

P.S I know others were worried about sending me because of my personality being quiet and a very clear introvert, but I am well-liked by the other host families for being polite. I have also made a great impression on Miss Suyeon Ahn and the people I have met. Even though my situation is different from the other exchange students considering I am a Korean American, we do share a lot of the same problems, stares, and popularity at school. I will try to message you again next month to let you know how I am doing.

November Letter

First of all, I would like to express my utmost and sincere thanks for letting me attend the Grant Management Seminar and Pre-PETS in Jackson on Oct 26. I admit there was an unsettling feeling and uneasiness on my part when I started writing letters to unknown faces back in August. Ever since I met you face to face, I do not feel I am writing to strangers anymore. Instead, I feel I am reconnected with old friends whom I have not seen for ages. Of course, I have not met all of you yet, but when you come to PETS (President Elect Training Seminar) on March 21 through 23, I hope you will feel the same as I have.

Today is Halloween. After work, I stopped at the Kroger and bought individually wrapped-assorted candies and hurriedly rushed home before gangs of trick-or-treaters knocked on the door. However, I noticed a little note taped on my front door saying that Trick-or-Treating was postponed to tomorrow due to the bad weather. As I turned the front porch light on, I was disappointed because I had to wait another day to become a child again, finding joy in the mere act of giving out candy. Since I was given an unexpected allotment of time, I scrolled through the television channels and a high speed, adrenaline rushing scene with familiar voices from a movie caught my eye.

It was the movie called "2012." The title of the movie attracted much attention when it was released in 2009, for it was based on the ancient Mayan prediction of the cataclysmic end of the world on December 21, 2012 which obviously did not happen. While watching the movie, I was swayed by the main character. In the movie, Jackson Curtis, played by actor John Cusack, is an unknown and struggling writer. He drives a limousine for a wealthy Russian family to make ends meet. He is divorced from his wife, and sold only one-hundred-twenty-two copies of his book, "Farewell Atlantis." Nothing was going well for him neither: his job, his family, nor his book. However, the climax of the movies, in my opinion, was how his book influenced Dr. Adrian Helmsley. Dr. Helmsley was a geologist and scientific advisor to the President of United States. The survival of the world solely depended on him. He happened to stumble on Jackson's book and said, "This book is a part of legacy now. You know why? It is because I am reading it." And in the end, he saved the world.

Jackson spent countless hours working on the book. If Jackson knew he would sell only a few hundred copies of his book, do you think he would have attempted to write a single paragraph? Do you think he knew that his book would save the world through just one of his readers? The point was not whether he became a best seller or not, it was his passion. That is why he followed his heart. He had no idea that his spark would become a fire that helped save the world.

I truly believe all of us have a fire within ourselves yearning for something in life. Some call it passion, love, or enthusiasm. Once we find that, it becomes our life long journey to keep it lit and to spread it. We, Rotarians, have such passion in our hearts. My passions may be different from yours, but that is what makes Rotary the best service organization in the world. I do not know what your passion is as the President of your club, but I am 100 % sure that you would find it in Rotary. It unites organizations and people like you and me who can work together to keep the fire lit. When we meet at PETS, I will ask each of the sixty-two President-elects to share their passions and how they are going to keep the fire lit so we can bring joy where there is sadness; hope where there is despair; light where there is darkness; love where there is hatred; and Rotary where there is no spirit of "Service Above Self." That is what Rotary is all about, and that is why we became Rotarians.

••

Dear Club President

I have pleaded with you since July in e-mails and monthly letters to select your club President for 2014-2015. Even District Governor, Judy Tyree, has mentioned in her newsletters numerous times that club must select President-elect, Club Secretary, and Foundation Chair for 2014-2015 by November 1, 2013. As a District Governor for 2014-2015, I feel I have failed your club President-elect for not giving him or her tools to succeed. I have longed to get to know your PE personally like I have known other PEs since July this year.

I should have communicated with you better. I should have emphasized more how important it is for your club to select President-elect so that he or she will be equipped and ready to take office in July 2014. On December 1, 2013, I have to submit names of all 62 President-Elects to Multi-PETS committee. Please email me by November 30 a name and contact information of your President-elect, or I have no other choice but to submit your name as President for 2014-2015.

Thank you for your understanding.

December Letter

I have written about my personal deployments as a member of the ShelterBox first disaster response team in my previous writings. I have had four deployments ever since I became a SRT (ShelterBox Response Team) member in 2009, and two of them were in the Philippines. Through this, the people of the Philippines came to have a very special place in my heart. The Philippines has a deep rooted Rotary history. Rotary first got involved with polio in 1979 when we committed ourselves to eradicate polio for six million children in the Philippines. It was how Rotary's Polio Plus program started worldwide in 1985. Also, I am a big fan of the world famous boxer Manny Pacquiao. My Filipino friends often post pictures with him on Facebook and brag about their projects. He is not only a congressman but the thirty-four year old president of the Rotary Club of Manila in 2013.

Ever since Haiyan, the most powerful typhoon ever recorded—370 miles wide with 235 mph winds—ripped through the Philippines on November 8, 2013, I felt an excruciating pain as if my own family was affected by the disaster. I could not stand as an idle bystander. I had to do something. In fact, I was not able to deploy to the Philippines due to my work and District Governor training, but I knew I could go to as many Rotary clubs as possible and speak about it.

I left home at 5:30 a.m. to attend Cookeville Breakfast Rotary Club, which meets at 7 a.m. Then, I drove two more hours to go to Fairfield Glade to speak to another Rotary Club and Interact Club. Those clubs were not even in my district, but as long as I was called to speak, I packed my ShelterBox demo box in the trunk of my car and appealed to the dire need in the Philippines and how we could help them through ShelterBox. Fairfield Glade Rotary Club gave me a check of $3,000 after my speech. A week earlier I attended Lawrenceburg Rotary Club. President Todd challenged his club members, and they instantly passed the hat and collected over $2,500. Also, I attended Nashville Rotary club to celebrate their 100 year anniversary, and they again made donations to ShelterBox. Many other Rotary clubs stepped up to the plate when needed. I was, once again, awed by Rotarians' generosity and big hearts. Rotarians always have risen to meet the immediate challenge and will be there to help rebuild their communities for years to come. Hence, our works just have begun in those affected communities.

I get the up-to-date e-mail from ShelterBox every day. The goal of ShelterBox is to provide enough shelters for 6,000 families. 13 million people have been affected by the typhoon, and our effort seems only a drop in an ocean. I remember my first deployment to the Philippines in 2009. When I arrived in Manila, there were 750,000 people displaced. Because of a lack of donations and because numerous countries were affected by different disasters at the same time, I was told that ShelterBox Headquarter could only send 200 Shelterboxes. Hearing that, I was not only disappointed but was furious after witnessing the dire situation that was worse than war. I cried out to the operation manager in Cornwell, England, "It is not going to make any difference with only 200 shelterboxes."

I felt that no matter what I did, it was not going to make any difference. It was a little Filipino child who changed me. But first, I need to tell the starfish story.

One day a man was walking along the beach. On a far distance, he saw a little girl bending down to pick something up on the sand and gently throw it into the ocean. As he approached, he saw hundreds of thousands of starfish. A little girl was picking up starfish one by one and throwing back into the ocean. He could not help but laugh. He said, "What are you doing, little girl?" She said, "the sun is up and the tide is going out. If I do not throw them back, they will die." He burst out laughing and said, "Do not you see there are miles and miles of beach and hundreds of starfish. It is no use. You can't possibly save them all!" After listening to him patiently, a little girl bent down, picked up another starfish and gently threw it into the ocean. Then, she smiled at the man and said, "I made a difference for that one."

When I visited one village in Laguna Bay area to set up tents, a little boy followed me everywhere I went in the rain. Out of curiosity, I asked him, "Where are your mom and dad?" Instead of answering my question, he ran into a young man who was helping me. So I asked a young man where his family was. A young man who appeared to be 16 or 17 year of age said, "He is my nephew. He had parents and two siblings. They all died." It became one of my personal rules in deployment never to ask where their families were, for I could not bear their answers.

The only thing I could think and do, right then, was to provide a tent for a little child so he could stay with his uncle's family. It was the heart-breaking process to select the most vulnerable people out of hundreds just like them. I used to think that the starfish story was a made-up story to teach us a lesson. I never imagined hundreds of thousands of stranded starfish were actual human beings. A man in a starfish story was I who thought it was no use trying to save because I could not possibly save them all. This little Filipino child taught me a life lesson to live one day at a time and to make a difference to one child at a time.

The most important lesson I learned at the worst situation was that even I could do something. I believe I have full potential and inborn talent from God. It is a gift from God, and I was born with it. How I am going to use it is a gift to God's people. If it were not for the challenges and obstacles I faced at the worst situation, I would have never realized my potential and talent that I have to become what I am meant to be.

Someone said, "The best and most beautiful things in the world cannot be seen or even touched; they must be felt with the heart." Thanks to a little Filipino boy, I could feel my heart, and it was beautiful thing.

January Letter

When I was a director of the hospital a few years ago, I had to submit 15 different reports to different departments each month. Needless to say, I did not quite understand what I had to do and why they were needed. I asked a former director why he had been doing it so redundantly. His answer was, "Frankly, I do not know. A director before me did it that way, so I have been doing what he always has done." So, one month, I decided not to submit any reports at all to see what happens. I spent many hours to finish all the reports just in case they all asked for them. Two months later, the finance department was the only one to call and asked for the particular report. What had happened to the other 14 monthly reports I had done for years? Nobody could explain to me why these reports had to be done every month, and I never filed those reports again.

Psychologist Harry Harlow conducted a series of experiments on monkeys behaviors to understand such human behavior. That experiment was called the five monkeys and the banana. Every time I hear someone say, "That's not the way we do things around here," or "That is how things are done around here," I ask "Why?" and tell them the monkey story.

Five monkeys are put into a cage, and in the middle a banana was hanging from the ceiling. The only way to get to the banana was to climb a step ladder which was placed right underneath the banana. Every time a monkey attempted to climb a step ladder to reach a banana, all five monkeys were sprayed with freezing water. After a few attempts, immediately followed by freezing water, all five monkeys learned not to climb a step ladder by avoiding the group punishment of being sprayed with freezing water.

Afterward, one of the monkeys was replaced with a new one. As soon as a new monkey saw a banana, he climbed the step ladder. Four other monkeys instantly jumped on him and beat him up repeatedly until he no longer climbed a step ladder even though he never knew why. A second monkey was replaced with a new one and the same thing happened. He climbed the step ladder and other monkeys including the first new monkey, who never experienced the freezing water, participated on the beating for second monkey as well. Third, fourth, and the fifth monkey were replaced one by one, and the same reaction repeated. Finally, all five monkeys were replaced. None of them was sprayed with freezing water but would not dare to climb a step ladder. Somewhere along the way, they learned they are not allowed to reach a banana even though they did not know why. In addition, they would beat up any monkeys who climbed the step ladder to reach a banana.

Does it sound familiar to you? Speaking of the matter, you might be dealing with a similar situation at work or in your Rotary club right now. We all have. Nevertheless, we continue doing what we have been doing even though there are different, new, and better ways of doing it. We not only repeat the same behavior over and over and expect the different results, but we protect the rule without truly knowing its purpose because it is a safeguard against unfamiliarity and intrusion. We want to be accepted and at the same time, we are not only resistant to change but object based mostly on the notion, "That is not how we used to do it," for we are afraid of failure. Therefore, we work hard to maintain and reinforce organizational culture that was created over the years.

I believe when a rule or a procedure is introduced for the first time, it has a valid reason at that time. Over the years, rules are changed and are no longer needed to meet their purposes, but we blindly follow and develop routines and habits. It gradually becomes common practices and unwritten rules in our organization. I am not saying old ways of doing things are all bad. What I am saying is we should be open minded and be aware of them so we can approach with new eyes and different mindsets. Charles F. Kettering once said, "People are very open-minded about new things—as long as they're exactly like the old ones." It is humorous, but we find it so true in some organizations.

How often do we hear that we must bring new, young, and vibrant members? We recognize that they are our blood line, and our future depends on them. Without them, there is not going to be Rotary. We say all those right words among ourselves. We recruit new members and expect them to fit into the culture we created. When they leave silently within six months to a year we say, "They are not fit to be Rotarians. The problem is them, not us."

I believe we have to re-examine our own club and its culture. Instead of pointing fingers to those members leaving and not engaging, we have to look into ourselves to see if we create the environment in which those qualified and potential members can blossom into servant leaders in Rotary. We truly believe Rotary has much to offer to any fellow human being who wants to live by our motto, "Service Above Self," no matter where they are, here in America or corners of Africa. That is why we remain passionate Rotarians. Why I joined Rotary is no longer a valid reason for why I stay in Rotary.

The good news is that you will be a president of your own club in July. You are holding the key to create such environment you want to see in the world. An unknown author once said, "Throughout the centuries, there were men who took first steps, down new roads, armed with nothing but their own vision." Do not let the mindset of "That's not the way we do things around here" stop you from doing something great. And ask "Why not?" Then, the only thing left to do is your action. We are born to be great. We should never be settled with mediocrity because somebody said, "We have done it before, and it does not work." So, what is it that prevents you from doing what you want to do?

In conclusion, I want to tell you another story. On Christmas Eve when the whole family gathers together, it has been a family tradition to cook a ham the night before. A granddaughter cut the end piece of the ham just like her mother had always done it and put it in the oven. It was perfectly good and the right size of ham. While making green bean casserole and other delicious dishes, she asks her mother with curious eyes why she has always cut the end piece of the ham. Mother says to her daughter, "I do not know, my dear. Your grandmother always has done it that way." So she turned around and asks her grandmother why. She says, "Your grandfather bought a ham that was too big to fit in a pan. So, I had to cut the end piece. Why are you cutting yours, dummy?"

February Letter

rotarian

    am

    malala

You have seen this already, haven't you? It was on the front cover of the January rotarian magazine. At first, I thought that it had to be a mistake or I was looking at the back cover. I turned it over, but it wasn't. On the white glossy front cover, there was nothing on it other than the name of the magazine. I instinctively murmured that something was not right. There was no captivating picture I have had seen each month or a simple but powerful single line drawing of a mother holding her baby in the December issue. I kept looking at it standing next to the mailbox on the cold wintry street. By the time I reached the front door, I completed the puzzle: underneath the letter "I" in the word, rotarian, it was written "am" and "malala" in red. But I did not know who Malala was.

I flipped through the second page and saw a 16 year old Pakistani school girl giving her book to Queen Elizabeth II in England. Even though her head and body was covered with a red veil, I knew right then, who she was. I have seen her face on the cover of Time magazine and heard about her inspiring and brave story numerous times in social media and CNN. Her story has captivated millions of people around the world and has become a beacon of hope and inspiration. The title of her book says it all, *I Am Malala: The Girl Who Stood Up for Education and Was Shot by the Taliban.*

However, that is not the reason why I am re-writing the story you as well as million people already know about. The intriguing story that I assume not many people know about, is that she is a daughter of a Rotarian. The rotarian magazine simply puts, "Malala is one of us." As a father of three children and as a fellow Rotarian, I could not be more proud of her and what she has become over night. Several months ago, I happened to listen to NPR (National Public Radio) interviewing her and her father. She said that she was inspired by her father. Her father, Ziauddin Yousafzaik, is an educator and activist who has spoken out women's right to education and empowerment even when the Taliban banned all girls from attending school. He has received many threats and assassinations from Taliban and taught his daughter to speak up for her right to get an education and go to school.

Ghanaian scholar Dr. Kwegyir Aggrey once said, "If you educate a man, you educate an individual. If you educate a woman, you educate a nation." I think that Rotarian Ziauddin has the same belief that if he educates women, they would become educated mothers, and educated mothers would educate their children for the next generation. In the interview with NPR, he said that he was often asked what he had done to raise such a brave and extraordinary 15 year old girl who was not afraid of speaking her mind and stood up against the Taliban. He said, "Malala is an average girl... You should not ask me what I have done. Rather you ask me, what I did not do." He continues, "I did not clip her wings to fly. I did not stop her from flying."

The relationship between Malala and her father reminds me of a Korean independence activist, Ahn Jung-geun and his mother. At the age of twenty-five, he established a private school and devoted himself to the education of Korean people under the Japanese colonial ruler. He was sent to a prison and waited to be executed. His mother received a letter from her son in jail saying he worried about her and he was sorry for dying before her. His mother wrote him back a stern letter, "If you think that dying before your mother is undutifulness to your parents, I would be a laughing stock. Your death is not yours. You are carrying the righteous indignation of the entire people. Do not beg for your mercy. Do not be afraid of death as you have done no wrong. Your brave death for justice is a final filial regard to your mother. "With this letter, she sent her loving son white silk Korean clothes to die in.

No parent should ever bury their sons and daughters before their own deaths. We bury them in our hearts, and we live with the pain and remorse that never leaves us until we die. So, it is the duty of us as parents to protect our children from harm and danger and provides warm, safe, and nurturing environment for them to grow. As a result of this unconditional or blind love for our children, we unwittingly disable them from becoming what they are meant to be. English Poet John Donne says, "No man is an island, entire of itself; every man is a piece of the continent, a part of the main.… Any man's death diminishes me, because I am involved in mankind; and therefore never send to know for whom the bell tolls; it tolls for thee."

In the name of protecting our precious children, we unintentionally clip their wings to fly and tell them to be silent and look the other way when they should stand up and take actions for what they believe in. Martin Luther King. Jr. said, "Our lives begin to end the day we become silent about things that matter." Because it is not our business, we ignore the dire need or rights of others; so we stand as idle bystanders. How can we do nothing when the other side of the wall catches fire? It becomes our business. Recently, I read Holocaust survivor, Elie Wiesel's book, "Night" and he said, "I swore never to be

132

silent whenever and wherever human beings endure suffering and humiliation. We must always take sides. Neutrality helps the oppressor, never the victim. Silence encourages the tormentor, never the tormented."

I do not remember if I told you this story in my previous writing or not. Even today, my wife does not exactly know what I do in my ShelterBox deployment. She thinks that like other Rotary international projects, I go and help people in a harm-free environment. I always felt I was protecting her from worries and doing her a favor. If she found out my real assignment, I was afraid she would never allow me to deploy again. So I decided it was better to keep her in the dark until my sister saw me on the CBS world news one evening. With people frantically escaping the disaster area, she saw me going in and being interviewed by BBC (the British Broadcasting Corporation). She immediately called my wife and asked, "What is my brother doing in disaster area in the foreign country?" Ever since then, my wife always worries, what if something happens to me, who is going to take care of our young children, our aging mother and all?

I have never told her that my truck collided head on with an incoming bus in the middle of deserted land, and I was hospitalized in the foreign country where a hospital they took me was a tent. Considering what I was called to do, it was really a minor accident compared to some of my team members who were being shot at. This is what I volunteer to do and will never stop saving lives until I am physically and mentally not fit to do so. At the same time, I painfully admit that I have been a hypocrite. This is my passion. I have never felt this strong about anything until I become a first disaster response team and after witnessing a difference I made to victims that lost everything they had. Nevertheless, I was not willing to allow my kids to go to such dangerous places to help them if they wanted.

I remember my father teaching me how to ride my bike when I was young. So, ever since my three kids started walking by themselves, they rode a tricycle at first. Later on, I taught them how to ride bikes the way my father taught me. I did it despite of how many times they fell and had bruises and cuts on their knees and arms. I encouraged them to get back on the bike and to try again and again every time they fell and cried. Since my kids are driving their own cars, I stayed up late and could not sleep until I see my kids come home safe from school and work at night. If I did not give them age appropriate responsibilities, I might not have to worry about them getting in accidents, but I crippled them for life and took away their right to fly, like a caged bird. What I have learned over the years from my mistakes and life experiences are risks, challenges, and obstacles are there to boldly face. They are by far worth more than avoiding it and more important than giving up. If it is right, I want my kids to "just do it," like a Nike commercial says, no matter what. Malala has a Rotarian father who acts upon what he believes in, and it is no surprise to see how Malala turns out to be, just like her father.

PART THREE

LETTERS FROM ROTARIANS

A Letter from Dave Black

Dear Fellow Rotarians,

I hope you have read the March 2008 issue of *The Rotarian* by the time you are reading this letter. The cover story about Dolly Parton and her Imagination Library should inspire all of us to make a greater difference. This is a story that touches us directly since the program started in Tennessee and is now spreading throughout the world to help children have a greater opportunity to read, learn and succeed. This issue tells how Dong Kurn Lee, who is Korean, will become the first Rotary International President for the term 2008-2009. His inspirational story is about a man self-described as a humble servant trying to make a difference.

This is obviously a situation that speaks to the smallness of the world in which we live. The *Tennessean,* Dolly Parton, and Korean Dong Kurn Lee are working to change the world for the better. They both represent what is special about our Rotary commitment of service to others for greater understanding and peace. They are both accomplishing this through attacking ignorance, poverty, and disease—the real enemies of peace for all nations. Each issue of *The Rotarian* is filled with stories of individuals participating in programs to help others wherever the need may exist.

One program that every Rotarian can support is the Paul Harris Fellowship which funds the many great works in progress throughout our troubled world. Not all of us have the ability to travel to some remote village or location in need, or leave our families or businesses to participate in a trip such as our annual mission trip to Guatemala, or have the financial resources to make a single large commitment in finances to travel to touch one specific person in need. We all do have the ability to commit to a Paul Harris Fellow, and over time, achieve the goal of a $1,000 donation to the Rotary Foundation to continue all the good works addressing hunger, disease, and health.

Diane and I became Paul Harris Fellows while our children were still young; therefore, our personal finances were strained by having three in college at the same time. However, we did also commit to financially support each of our children to become Paul Harris Fellows by donating small amounts over time. Our giving was erratic and the goal was not achieved in the original planned time frame. But the ultimate commitment was there. and we have achieved what we started by having supported six Paul Harris Fellows. We do intend to continue to add to our contributions, because there is so much that is accomplished through Rotary throughout the world.

The second obvious part of the story of Rotary International President Dong Kurn Lee is our Hendersonville Rotary President, Kim Kim , for the same Rotary year of 2008-2009. I suspect we may be the only club in the United States whose Rotary President is our first Korean. Fortunately Kim is from "South" Korea and not one of those darn Yankee Koreans. But would it not be a great accomplishment and honor for our two Korean Presidents to achieve 100% Paul Harris Fellowship participation for our club during their term? It would honor not only them but also our club Rotarians who I believe represent the world's greatest Rotary Club.

Thanks for reading,

A Letter from Kara Arnold

Dear Fellow Rotarians:

I hope you have been as touched as I have by Kim Kim's letters each month. After 3 or 4 of them, I started to wonder how he could be so passionate about something to consistently reach out, month after month, to all 120 or so of us. Many times after someone has done something especially selfless I think of how I will put a card in the mail or at least send an email letting that person know how sincerely grateful I am. Then a week passes, another week, and yet another and no card has been sent. It's not that I intentionally put it off, but I get caught up in all the important things and events in my life and I forget to reach out and share with that person how he/she made me feel. Sometimes I do not send that note because sincere words are hard to find, and, once written down, they just do not seem to convey my true feelings. Or perhaps I do not send the note because sharing true feelings, even ones of gratitude, can bring vulnerability and discomfort.

Regardless of the why, when it comes to sharing how we feel with others it is easier not to act. For this reason I am compelled to read Kim Kim's notes every month, and I am greatly moved after doing so. How could I read these letters and not give?

If there were an award in Rotary for the member who could least afford to give $1,000, I would certainly be up for the vote. My husband and I are still young in our careers (Eric Jackson, if you're reading this, that's my way of saying you do not pay my husband enough); we have a toddler at home who is huge and eats a ton; and we're renovating an older home in Nashville and can't wait to move back to Sumner County. Not to mention, I work for a nonprofit organization that I am passionate about, and to which I feel compelled to give. And my brother is the campus minister for RUF at SMU, and I think I'm expected to give to him, too.

Trust me, there's a laundry list of reasons not to give to Rotary International. I will compare it to having a baby. If you wait until you feel like you're ready to have a baby before having one, you'll never do it because a person is never truly ready to have a baby. But isn't the ROI worth it (as a mom I would say 'definitely')? Some of us will never feel like we're financially secure enough to just give our money away, and that's because we're not. True financial security is a myth because life is full of the unexpected. And that's where faith comes in, no matter what you put your faith in. It takes some faith just to get through the day with any degree of enjoyment. It takes faith to let go of $1,000 and know that it will come back to you in some form.

I remember when I was 16 and brought home one of my first paychecks from working the concession stand at the Grand Ole Opry. My mom encouraged me to tithe, but writing that check for $35 every 2 weeks started to get old. After several months I added up what I had given, and it seemed like so much money. I could not believe I had just given all that money away. I decided tithing wasn't for me—I was actually raised Catholic anyway, and they never mentioned tithing. My mom noticed the next Sunday after payday when I did not put anything in the collection plate. She did not scold me or force me to give. She simply said, "It's always hard to give money away, and it's always easier to say that you will give a lot someday when you are rich and have so much to spare. But if you can't let go of it when you have a little, it will only be harder to let go of it when you have more." It's funny that I remember that since it made no sense to me at the time. But I put my faith in her words and I gave. And now, as an adult with a job that pays more than $350 every 2 weeks, I understand what she meant. Giving away money is no easy task. My mom wanted me to practice so that when the time came and I had more money and more responsibilities and more expenses, letting go of something I may feel I need would come naturally. After all, there are always those who need it more.

It also feels good to give, just look at the joy and passion that giving to this mission has brought our fellow Rotarians— Kim Kim, David & Diane Black, S.T. & Mary Ann Womeldorf, Art McClellan, Brenda Payne, Bill Sinks, etc. That's a group that I believe I want to be a part of. I love being a part of our Rotary Club. I love knowing that I am a part of something bigger than just myself. And I am looking forward to the day when I do become a Paul Harris Fellow and will then also be connected to Rotary International, to a family that spans the globe. If you decide to give, you may find that it brings you such joy that you just want to give some more. If this becomes the case, feel free to make your tax-deductible donation to COMPASS once you have become a Paul Harris Fellow.

Thank you for reading my story.

Family Connection Makes Real

Over the past several months, I have read with great pride the letters from several of my Rotary buddies about their commitment to the Rotary tradition of Paul Harris Fellowship. Kim Kim has encouraged all of us to participate in this Rotary mission and specifically several of us to communicate by letter to our members. The letters to date have been eloquent, personal and have offered compelling reasons for each of us to become a part of this worldwide fellowship.

Giving is such a personal matter and the reasons behind these personal decisions are as numerous as each of us. It is not possible for me to know how you might be touched. My reason for writing this letter is not to motivate you to make this an important decision, as it is to complete a commitment to my good friend, Kim. I also hope that sharing this insight with you may help us know each other better; isn't that what Rotary is all about?

I joined our club in March, 1995, at the invitation of my good friend Pat Lebkuecher. I guess she thought I might be a good representative to replace Jim Moore, my late husband, from Volunteer State Community College. I am sure over the next few years I must have heard about Paul Harris Fellow, but it was not until I learned more about Polio Plus and the matching grant program that I began to seriously think about a $1,000 gift to the Rotary Foundation.

You see, my first cousin Mike Bingham (who is my age), was struck by polio while we were small children. He was the one in his family of 5 children who sat on the sidelines with his big grin, while we played softball or kickball at family reunions. He was the one who stayed skinny from all the extra exertion to get around. He was the one who married, had children, worked full time, never complained and always had his big grin when I saw him. He was the one, who after 40 years of living with the same routine, is now experiencing new symptoms associated with the acute disease we believed he fought and overcame as a child.

My first gift of $1,000 was matched, becoming $2,000 to fight polio worldwide. My second gift, to honor Jim Payne, was given after having the privilege to go to Guatemala and realizing what a small world we live in and how these dollars can go so far. Rotary International is now partnering with the Bill and Melinda Gates Foundation to match gifts to a total of $100,000,000, which means a huge infusion of new money to battle polio. I know my gift will make a difference in the future of another child with a big grin and I hope when you close your eyes, you can see a big grin too.

Sincerely,

Brenda Payne

Service Above Self

Service above self is a precept of Rotary that has inspired men and women worldwide to give their resources and time to help others. The world is a better place as the result of efforts of Rotarians. Pause to think of the countless children worldwide that are enjoying a polio-free life today because of Rotary's efforts to eradicate this disease. We are changing the world. Part of this transforming the world begins in Hendersonville, Tennessee. As the Hendersonville Rotary Club celebrates its 40th anniversary, I reflect back on my 15 years as a member of the club.

Forty years ago a small group of Hendersonville businessmen had a vision of making their community a better place to raise their children by giving something back to the community. Perhaps they reflected on the scripture of "Unto whom much is given, much is required," and determined that forming a Rotary club would provide them the opportunity to serve others in the small but promising community of Hendersonville. Their names may be unknown to us today but their deeds will never be forgotten and their legacy is what our club has become today. I did not have the privilege of knowing many of these founders but our community is far better for their efforts and our club today is the product of their dreams and aspirations. I came to join our club many years later in 1994. This is my story of how I came to join our club and what the club means to me.

The year 1994 for me was, as Dickens would say, the best of times and the worst of times. It was this year that my mother passed away after fighting for over 10 years the ravages of heart disease. But it was also the year that I joined the Hendersonville Rotary Club and was offered the opportunity to make a difference. One reason I joined our club was the example that my mother set for me. My mother was an orphan at the age of 8 due to her parents' death. Many years later, while still at the orphanage, she met my father in a church service in Cleveland, Tennessee and following a brief romance, were married. Shortly thereafter my father was called into the ministry and they began a life of service to God by serving their fellow man. Vividly, I recall growing up in the church parsonage with the constant stream of individuals knocking on our door asking for assistance. It was usually my mother that greeted the individuals. And while I was often skeptical of the hard luck stories these people told my mother, while I was hiding behind her apron, she was never judgmental but always kind and willing to do whatever she could to meet their need. Whether it was a dollar bill or a sandwich, a piece of fruit or a fried pie, my mother gave what she had and her life exemplified service above self. I do not know how many people may have taken advantage of my mother's generosity, but I have never doubted for one moment that many were touched by her kindness and only eternity will be able to tally the fruits of her unselfish actions. From an early age, she taught me that the greatest gift a Christian could give would be to offer assistance to someone down on their luck. She lived this creed until her last days. No wonder it was estimated to be one of the largest visitations of any funeral at the funeral home. It was always someone else that was the focus of her attention: her family, her friends, her church, her community. These seeds planted deep within me as a child have given me the opportunity to grow as an adult as a member of the Hendersonville Rotary Club.

While still mourning the death of my mother, I determined to carry on her example of service above self by becoming more active in my local church and by joining a civic club dedicated to the same principle. My survey of civic clubs in Hendersonville did not take long. I reached out to the Hendersonville Rotary Club and was invited to join. I was welcomed with open arms and immediately became involved with the scholarship committee. I will never forget the letters of deserving high school students seeking our clubs assistance in order to attend college and the immense satisfaction of awarding, on behalf of the club, scholarships. Later, I was elected to the Board of Directors of the club and saw more clearly the scope of our club's benevolence and our members' big hearts and generous spirits. While our focus is mainly meeting the needs of local charities, our club's humanitarian reach is worldwide. From the tsunami victims of the Far East to the children of Guatemala, to the prevention of polio in India and Africa, our club's efforts are felt. We are changing the world and I am glad to be a small part of the effort. I believe my mother would be pleased.

In 2005, I received one of the highest honors of my life. Then president-elect Brenda Payne asked me to consider running my name for President of the club. At first, I was reluctant doubting my qualifications and my ability to lead our club. But during my deliberation of my decision, I kept thinking of my mother and her example and the wonderful opportunity the position would afford me to work with other Rotarians to fulfill our club's creed and society's need. How could I refuse the call? What an experience! Being club president helped me better understand the potential of our club and passionate motivation of club members. Our club is great because of its members and their common belief in Rotary's Four-Way Test. And while I am sure I made mistakes and unintentionally offended individuals while president, the experience gave me much more than I could have ever given. As I gave my closing remarks as president, I stressed how much we have done in the past and how much more we can do in the future if we stay united and committed to changing the world. Now is not the time to rest on our laurels but forge ahead to meet the new pressing needs in our community and world. More than ever before, our community needs the influence and impact of our Rotary Club.

One of the most profound examples of service above self of our club is the experience of Doran Lee. Doran was a recipient of Cultural Ambassadorial Scholarship from South Korea to our area the year I was president. One night in November of 2007, she was involved in a terrible car accident. Her life hung in the balance for many days. Her family was thousands of miles away and it appeared that she was all alone. I recall Kim Kim calling me the night of the accident and asking what our club can do to help Doran. At the very next Rotary meeting, I put forward the need and the response of the club was overwhelming. Under the direction of Secretary Robin Williams, over $10,000 was raised to help the Lee family cope with the situation. The rest of the story is good. Doran survived the ordeal and is back at home in South Korea preparing to live the rest of her life as a healthy young lady. Doran now states that as soon as she gets out of school that she wants to join a Rotary club in South Korea to repay back the kindness she received from the Hendersonville Rotary Club in her most desperate hour of need.

I thank the Hendersonville Rotary Club for providing me the means to fulfill my mother's challenge to put service to others above self. You have changed the lives of many and the best is yet to come.

Eddie Roberson

Dedication to S.T. Womeldorf
1936 – 2009

Hendersonville Rotarian Stephen Thomas "S.T." Womeldorf passed away on May 19, 2009, at the age of 73. S.T. was a living example of the Rotary motto, "Service Above Self." He worked tirelessly, diligently and often anonymously to make our world a better place to live.

Since joining the Hendersonville Rotary Club in August 1982, S.T. exemplified Rotary service. He served as President in 1993-94 and was Assistant District Governor for District 6760. S.T. received the Lifetime Distinguished Service Award at the end of the 1999-00 year, and was named Rotarian of the Year for his work during the 2000-01 year. He was a Paul Harris Fellow and Major Donor who honored every member of his family with a Paul Harris Fellowship, including his last grandchild in 2009. For S.T., one of the most important acts of service was simply showing up—his 26 years of perfect attendance at Rotary Club meetings proves it.

S.T. always showed up for others, generously sharing his time and talents with those in need. He spent six years on the board of Second Harvest Food Bank, where he also chaired and served on the Distribution Committee. He was one of the founders and Past President of Nashville's Table, served as Past President and Board Member of the Community Child Care Services, and was a Board Member of Right Turns.

Many of S.T.'s favorite Rotary projects benefitted children. He was an integral member of the Guatemala Mission team and participated in ten mission trips. He worked for years to fill a container with thousands of dollars worth of medical equipment and supplies, which was sent to Guatemala in 2008. He was actively involved in the *Wheels in Motion* project and mentored young people at local elementary schools.

S.T. could always spot potential. He provided love and encouragement to people of all ages, and was also the consummate Rotary recruiter. His quiet enthusiasm inspired many to get involved. At least 22 current members of the Hendersonville Rotary were recruited by S.T. and he sponsored more than 100 new members in his lifetime.

For S.T., "Service Above Self" wasn't about helping others and then secretly hoping for credit; it was about seeing a need and showing up to meet it with little discussion and absolutely no fanfare. He did not want attention. He just wanted to give.

This is why the Rotary Club of Hendersonville dedicates its 40th anniversary publication to S.T. Womeldorf. His life represented all that is noble and honorable. He will be missed.

Gayla Zoz

What's a Rotary?

I'm always amazed when someone asks me, "What's a Rotary?"
A question asked by a kid, young adult, or a contemporary.

I realize that sometimes my answers might be short and brief.
It depends on the time, and place, my attitude, and my belief.

We all have newspapers, television, and the worldwide internet.
It's amazing the rotary abc's elude the communication connect.

I do not know when or where, but I know I'll "rehear" that question.
I may reply, "World's oldest, best, and largest service organization."

I've been asked several times, "What is a service organization?"
Rotary is the world's best secret, until you've had the conversion.

If we do not focus and share, we may limit the rotary choices.
When clubs continue to grow, it gives our membership new voices.

Our Rotary numbers are growing. We read it in the headline!
But our membership in the U.S.A. continues its slow decline.

Some clubs in our District, just seem to have lost their glow.
But meanwhile, Rotary of Hendersonville continues to grow.

It is certainly not because we have done it all by the book.
Our city is still growing and there is a prosperous outlook!

We surely are very fortunate that we can continue to expand,
During the time when some clubs are planning to disband.

So what are the four avenues of service, you may ask?
It's the way we organize committees and delegate our tasks.

Many of Rotary's service efforts are carried out at the club level.
Rotary international & District 6760 provide counsel.

Over the years I've been asked many times, much to my chagrin,
"Is that lapel pin you're wearing some kind of a fancy church pin?"

"I am a rotarian from Hendersonville. I'm also a Presbyterian."
"So what is it? You're some kind of a vegetarian?"

We moved from Virginia to Nashville around thirty years ago.
Mary Anna, our three daughters, S.T. and his five-string banjo.

We selected Hendersonville, after doing some strategic research,
And we moved our membership to the First Presbyterian Church.

The first Sunday at our new church, I was invited to join the choir.
That day I met Ralph Hanning and I discovered a very live wire!

We had an excellent choir, although some were a little Bohemian.
Ralph Hanning, John Park, and I took turns at playing comedian.

Some months later, Ralph invited me to a rotary breakfast.
Ralph did this regularly with folks; he was a recruiting enthusiast.

Ralph said, "We do not do roadblocks, sell light bulbs, or brooms.
Some think dues are a little high but just watch as our club blooms!"

Ralph brought many potential members into this "four-way" flow.
He felt every member was responsible for helping our club to grow.

Ralph Hanning set a recruiting example for the rest of us to follow.

The "King" brought more folks into our club than anyone else I know.

He selected, he trained and sometimes held your hand!
He tried to keep it simple, so we all could understand.

Ralph brought in four "recruits" who were all inducted the same day.
One of those four beautiful ladies was our twenty sixth President, Rae!

Rae Collier is closing in fast on Ralph. She'll be our recruiting queen.
I certainly do not have a list of them all but it's several times umpteen!

Past president, Bill Taylor, set a big goal for thirteen new members.
I told Bill I could recruit that many and started with my maneuvers.

I only brought in twelve that year. Many thought that was pretty neat.
They are not all in our club today. Some just lost the Rotary heartbeat.

I pay more attention now to a tactic that rotarians call retention.
If we properly train our recruits it might help change their perception.

Some down through the years, may have "unlearned" orientation.
We do not always apply the rules and a few "do not like" that connection.

Signing our Charter in sixty nine, we agreed to the rotary plan.
Not just for the original signers, but for each and every rotarian.

Rotary has everything laid out. If we follow it, we won't "misdeal."
Occasionally some well-meaning members want to "reinvent the wheel."

We have an awesome organization, when everyone does his part.
But sometimes it seems our best efforts get the horse behind the cart.

Rotary provides us the plan and a procedure for changing the rules.
If we will all just follow this plan, we won't look like bumbling fools.

Every member should have an active buddy, or they may not survive.
Miss the attendance requirement, and you might fail to thrive!

Rotary International recently adjusted the old attendance rule.
Some of our Rotary members now believe that fifty percent is cool!

"Why care about district 6760 or rotary international?"
You'll miss some great fellowship. The experiences are exceptional!

"Why do you give to Polio Plus and that Rotary Foundation?"
"Why not use some of that money right here in our local organization?"

"Somehow I've never felt of Hendersonville as a third world country."
"Many of us should feel lucky to be prospering in Middle Tennessee."

When we joined there was no agreement to only help folks in our state.
If we can help some kids in Guatemala, I'm hoping we'll accommodate.

My Uncle John, a Presbyterian minister, contracted polio as a kid.
He always walked with a limp and could not do what the others did.

During the fifties, our family stood in line for that polio vaccine.
It was mom, dad and me, and two sisters, Joanne and Emojeane.

We'd heard that it was coming, this crippling and killing machine!
And my lingering questions about polio were anything but routine.

There was an unusual quiet that day; it was more like a church event.
Everyone seemed consumed that day with a quiet bewilderment.

The unasked questions went unanswered. Some felt like a castaway.
Everyone dealt with his own concerns. Today it's a foggy yesterday.

We survived that scare in the fifties. Now we're glad it's them, not us.

We're sure it will all blow over in time, no point in making a fuss!

A rotarian from district 6760 showed us a film on Polio Plus.
I saw scenes of "the crawlers," and got on the Paul Harris bus!

Shouldn't all rotarians strive to make this old world a better place?
It takes a small part of your budget but an extra large dose of grace.

Anyone who donates $10,000 or more to the Rotary Foundation
Will be known as a major donor in this world wide organization.

We must know in this day and time that we can't keep it over there.
If we can't "nip it in the bud," this disease could spread everywhere.

Rotary International teamed up with the World Health Organization.
How can we miss with partners like the Bill Gates connection?

Who, but Rotary, could conceive such a goal and put that plan in place?
Numerous volunteers are involved. It's one goal we all can embrace.

Brenda Payne is totally involved. She inspires volunteers to appear!
The year she was president; we won district club of the year!

Our President, Kim Kim's goals is concise and crystal clear.
Just last year, Kim was selected as District Rotarian of the year!

Kim is one of a small group trained for the ShelterBox program.
He is a well respected Rotarian and he's a dedicated family man.

Todd Odum was president and encouraged members to take ownership.
Hendersonville won District Project of the Year under his leadership.

Don Ames and Michael Clark have visions for Festival by the Lake.
To be successful at this event every year, takes a lot of give and take.

Past President James Vandiver was a wonderful speaker and pastor.
It was only a few years later, that he became our District Governor.

Leading our most successful fundraiser is Billy Sinks, the man.
He and his helpers assign a time and place for every Rotarian.

"Why do you go every year on that Guatemala mission trip?"
"A lot of kids in Sumner could qualify for some dental hardship."

I agree there are kids and grownups, who need our help everywhere.
But Sumner County's needs are small, compared to those down there.

Dianne and David worked with Bill Taylor to start this mission trip.
Some others were also involved in this effort, including Pat and Rip.

When our dental trips were started, I'd say, "Well, maybe next year."
Our daughter, Becky, adopted Isabella, and I got my hinny in gear!

It's amazing how far a dollar will go in a country like Guatemala!
Their water supply is so polluted; we all have to drink bottled agua.

Guatemala is a beautiful country that has been ravaged by civil war.
The country is made up of a few rich men and multitudes of the poor.

After fifty political activists were killed during a bloody defection,
Guatemalans came out in droves to vote in the Presidential Election.

Guatemala is one of Latin America's most violent and unfair countries.
Governments filled with folks, who do not appear to have many remedies.

The country of Guatemala is about the size of our own Tennessee.
It borders El Salvador, Mexico, Honduras, and the Caribbean Sea.

Mountains make up much of the country, in those western highlands.
The Pacific Coast, on the western side, borders some very fertile lands.

They have the black sand beaches, and waterfalls that are amazing!
There are always active volcanoes in the lands of Eternal Spring.

They have beautiful mountains, surrounding some breathtaking lakes.
You might consider retiring there but for earthquakes and the snakes.

Guatemala's capital is a metropolis, known as Guatemala City.
Thirteen million people live in the country, in an uneasy fraternity.

They live in houses, shacks, lean-tos, and big mansions on the hill.
Many live on the streets of the city, looking for work, food or a pill.

They also live in cardboard boxes at the dump in Guatemala City.
They dig daily through the "treasures" and still maintain their dignity.

Family groups and other vagabonds recycle in this offensive cavity.
Selling their "finds" at the end of the day; they do not want your pity!

It's a good day when no one is killed or hurt by a filthy garbage truck.
To survive this grisly situation, requires determination, skill, and luck!

Most of our flights to Guatemala City are crowded but uneventful.
There are plenty of kids aboard, who are inquisitive and delightful!

There've been no chickens on the planes, the way some do on the bus.
We're a closely-packed family. There are lots of them and a few of us.

Our landing is somewhat unusual. Their runway is tilted downhill!
The pilot approaches the high side. We pray for brakes and goodwill!

Baggage claim is another story. Twelve folks want to tote your bag!
But first you have to locate them, in the "Under Construction" zig zag.

Marco will be there to meet us, but he's always on Guatemalan time.

It does not have to make sense to us, neither the reason nor the rime.

Our destination is a downtown motel, in cars or some age-old bus.
This "Annual Re-initiation" brings back memories for all of us.

The motel is another reality check, and we line up there to sign in.
The sign says "Express Check In!" The locals look at us and grin

That night we walk a few blocks on the bustling streets downtown.
We order food and have a drink and hope that this meal stays down.

Sometime later we walk back "home" and attempt to get some sleep.
I toss and turn most of the night not bothering to "count the sheep."

Early the next morning they set out cereal, fruit, and coffee downstairs.
We can smell the diesel truck fumes as we sit in those rickety chairs.

We load up supplies and equipment and start off to our workplace.
The school bus is fifty years old but is driven by a Guatemalan ace!

We face wall-to-wall traffic and diesel fumes, in this "creeping" rat race.
Motorcycles dart in and out. The bus lurches, at a stop and go pace.

Arriving at the Remar School, we're thankful for our "safe passage."
We unload and set up the equipment and display our dental image.

We usually set up only twice a week, but we have done this every day.
But we can lose a lot of valuable time with this "hit and run" relay.

The kids all line up to watch us, from outside the chain link fence.
Everyone wants to be first in line and they push with confidence.

The Guatemalans stand in line to spend time in the dental chair.
We give them soap, shampoo, and toys with a little gringo fanfare.

They are thankful for what we bring, though there never is enough.
We usually manage to run out and that's just another kind of tough.

We stop by the store on our way back "home" to supper and our beds.
And purchase more soap for their bodies and shampoo for their heads.

Jason and Rip discuss asking the board for extra money next year.
We do not have enough assistants; we could use another volunteer.

Guatemala has the prettiest, dirty little kids that you will ever see.
We are just like a circus to them, "Those gringos from Tennessee!"

Our dentists have the impossible job. They can't "repair" every kid.
It's back-aching work for them. Sometimes the conditions are lurid!

Jason and Bill keep all of us motivated, cracking comments every day.
Much of our "assisting" is a joke. We just try to stay out of their way.

In order to bail us out, Bill usually brings along some of his staff.
It is easy to see the difference, between the wheat and the chaff.

They provide this backbreaking work, to those kids, all week long.
You cannot keep up with them, although I am a bit headstrong.

Bill Taylor and Jason Tabor are my heroes on the mission trip.
They work under negative conditions on this dental apostleship.

The people in line just watch us, as they patiently wait their turn.
As the long line slowly advances, they begin to show more concern.

When it comes time for the chair, they will have mixed reactions.
They sit like statues, or will not be still awaiting their corrections.

They leave the chair crying or smiling, with a mouth full of cotton.
Getting your teeth fixed in Guatemala must feel like a marathon.

Several years ago in Zacapa, we watched some kids playing soccer.
They challenged us to a game, but we would not have had a prayer.

These kids were playing with a rock, wrapped up in a burlap sack!
They were playing a fantabulous game. They could really attack!

We went to the village that night and purchased a new soccer ball.
The next day these kids turned pro. Everyone played six feet tall!

We went to a café for supper and observed an "opossum in flight!"
It fell down through the ceiling and on a table nearby, it did light.

The waiters took off their aprons and ushered that intruder outside.
Although the food was average, we observed the floorshow ringside!

Every year's trip is different, though we may have been there before.
We set up in churches, clinics or schools. Some have had a dirt floor.

We would work until it was dark, pack up and head down the road.
Then we'd drive the crooked roadways back to our nighttime abode.

It's a whirlwind pace every year, although much of our work is slow.
There's a day at the lake or the beach and we'll head home tomorrow.

Rotarian and Lion, Milton Curtis, started an unlikely partnership.
He has the Lions collecting glasses for us to take on our mission trip.

Each year we provide glasses, partnering with Volunteer State.
The optometry students and the eye doctor work hard to elucidate.

Four students will go this year to be supervised by a local eye doctor.
We have twenty-eight folks going this time to help with our endeavor!

Here at home we have collected hospital supplies and equipment.

Phil Kile always loans us a truck from his rental establishment.

We picked up and stored supplies and all the donated equipment.
In December, we loaded a container and then trucked it to a ship.

We loaded this container for Guatemala on a cool December day.
This ended several years of hard work, as we shipped it on its way.

Those beds and other durables, would wind up in our scrap yard.
Folks in Guatemala make good use of the things that we discard.

Before you ask the question, a container is tractor trailer in size.
The kind we share the road with as we drive the days of our lives.

People say time flies. We're planning to celebrate forty years.
My most heartfelt thanks go out to all our Rotary volunteers!

A highlight of Rotary for me was my invitation to Kim Kim.
Rotary becomes a better organization with new members like him.

I am sure my Rotary legacy will continue through Kim Kim.
Some day, when I finally grow up, I want to be more like him!

S.T. Womeldorf

What Rotary Means to Me

For someone who never intended to become a "Rotarian", I am surprised at how much Rotary has come to mean to me.

I joined Rotary merely as a byproduct of being so heavily involved in the Career Network program co-sponsored a number of years ago by the City of Hendersonville, the Chamber, the Pastor's Association and Rotary.

As the HR Manager for the City, I was assigned by then Mayor Hank Thompson the task of assisting with the launch of Career Network as well as to provide ongoing support every Tuesday night. This arrangement lasted for a number of years.

During that time, I came in contact with many Rotary members who were the most dedicated volunteers with whom I enjoyed working with. Witnessing their degree of commitment as weekly program facilitators was impressive. Through their behavior, I grew to appreciate the depth of service to the community that Rotary provided. They truly exemplified "service above self".

Rotary provided the funding for the postage and supplies needed by Career Network as well as the majority of volunteers. Before I even belonged to Rotary, I felt a kinship. It was an honor to be invited by David Cooper, one of my co-facilitators, to join Rotary.

To be honest, I wasn't sure that I was going to like Rotary, but I thought I would give it a try. Not being a morning person, I dread that early call of the Wednesday morning alarm. I'm usually in a four way race in the parking lot to not be the last in. Rotary is a learning process: I have learned not to wear high heels and narrow skirts that limit your stride. I have also learned that timing is everything. My late arrivals usually coincide with a new batch of scrambled eggs being replenished on the buffet table; the cooked oatmeal at that point is not an option. Trying to sing, pray and pledge allegiance while standing with plate and coffee cup in hand is not fun either, nor is trying to chase Don Ames around the room to find the sign in sheet. I'm glad I finally memorized the four way test since I can't see it from my latecomer's hall of "shame" spot.

What's even worse is that I probably have the shortest distance of anyone in the club to travel to our meeting.

Once seated, the first fifteen minutes of Rotary are a blur for me until the caffeine kicks in. Fortunately, no one has asked me about my buddy for the past two years. This is good, because on any given morning, I probably haven't checked out the place to see where my buddy is nor would I be able to come up with the snappy and witty repartee that most of my fellow Rotarians manage to the great amusement of all. My best shot would be to mutely hand over my penalty dollar.

I look forward to our programs every week. (I am usually awake by then.) Without fail, they expand my concept of my community, whether that is global or local.

I often find myself later talking about the programs to friends and family. A case in point: About a year ago, I sent a dear friend, who was bemoaning her newly empty nest, to Gene Brown Elementary to be a mentor. She did not just mentor one little girl; she has two now that she just "loves". The other day I overheard her talking to a mutual friend, a newly retired school teacher about the mentoring program. Hopefully her enthusiasm lit a fire in yet another volunteer.

If I hadn't learned of the program at Gene Brown at Rotary, there would not have been this connection. This is what I love about Rotary. The organization sparks a broad spectrum circle of influence that can range from a worldwide polio eradication program to the micro level of making a difference in the lives of several local children.

As busy as we all are, it is so easy to fall into the tunnel vision of our daily routines. The programs at Rotary help me really see beyond the privileged life of suburbia that I take for granted.

The four way test speaks volumes about Rotary. This creed impresses me every time I hear and say it. This gold standard of behavioral expectations hopefully inspires members to be model citizens of our community in every aspect of their lives. I have never belonged to an organization previously (other than church) in which the mission statement was spoken aloud on a regular basis. This constant reminder of who we are or should be is something I respect and value greatly.

I also enjoy the camaraderie of Rotary as it provides an opportunity for me to make acquaintances and friends outside of my work and church interests. I had no networking agenda when I joined Rotary. I do not have a business; I wasn't running for political office and I had plenty of good friends and interesting activities already in my life when I joined.

Rotary truly had to be a "value added" experience when I put it to the test of whether I wanted to invest my time and money in the organization. Eight years later, I still think of Rotary as a good deal on both counts.

Sincerely,
Kaye Palmer

A Letter from Rod Lilly

Throughout my life, I have tried to give to others and serve my community. From High School, when I was in the Rotary affiliate, seeing the expression of thanks from serving people in need has been a source of personal satisfaction. "Service above Self" is a way life in Rotary.

In 1994 when I finished a consultant job, I was determined to give something back to Hendersonville and Sumner County instead of spending my efforts in Nashville/Davidson County. The Hendersonville Rotary Club was doing good work and I knew several members. I went to Lewis Oliver, who was President and asked for an application, which Randy Stamps signed as a sponsor. I thank both of these men and the Club for allowing me the opportunity to be of service.

There is no better way to be involved in your hometown than to help others and to be part of an organization which seeks to serve others. As a transplant from Virginia, the kindness and friendships I have in Rotary mean very much. After years of witness to my brother in Norfolk, he joined Rotary and I have had the pleasure of attending his club with him.

At times in our lives, problems and other commitments can cause us to be less active than we would like to be. That happened to me last year, but I am rededicating myself to the work of Rotary...Service Above Self. When I could not achieve

100% attendance last year, it was a wakeup call for me to work harder.

This year with Kim Kim as President and RI President Lee's theme of "Making Dreams Real" I have been invigorated in my desire to serve. The joy seen in Kim Kim as he continues to serve others makes the motto real for me. The testimony of a mother of two who continued with her dream of a college education at Volunteer State because Rotary cared enough to give a scholarship makes real the hope Rotary give to others.

May the Hendersonville Morning Rotary Club continue to make a difference in the lives of its members as well as the people of Hendersonville, Sumner County and the WORLD.

A Letter from Jim Campbell

Almost sixty years ago I attended what I thought was a Rotary Club outing with my parents in Michigan. It was on a farm out in the country with many animals, and as I recall, some booths selling homemade baked goods, probably a fund raiser.

As I walked along amazed at everything, I looked down and saw two one dollar bills just sitting there, and as I picked them up I felt the presence of a giant man in dark blue attire standing right in front of me. YES, it was the LAW and I'd better be on my best behavior. He asked me what I had there and what I was going to do with the money. I have always been a quick thinker, and being on my best behavior, I told him that I was going to turn the money in to see who lost this money. He took the money, my name and address, and promised that if no one claimed it, he would return it to me.

After about two weeks, I figured that my newly found fortune was gone forever, but that afternoon I received a very nice letter and the two dollars enclosed from the policeman, thanking me for being so honest. That was my first taste of Rotary and the police force. At that point I realized that they were both there to serve the community.

When we moved to Hendersonville in 1989, a friend and business competitor, Larry Johnson invited me to come to a Rotary Club meeting. I'd known Larry since 1974 when we were living in Knoxville, and I was working for General Motors: he was always a great person. I retired from GM in 2002 and later took a part time job to keep my sanity. I thought maybe now I had time for other activities so with Larry's urging I joined in

2003. However, I only wished that I had joined many years earlier when I was young more able to take part in all of the many activities.

The most important segment of Rotary is of course the people, and this Club has many, many ALL- STARS. Kim Kim has been a driving force in uniting people and was the major force in my being a "Paul Harris Fellow." In many years I have never known someone so dedicated to his cause/causes and an inspiration to us all.

Thank you Larry Johnson and Kim Kim, and thank you Rotary Club for being an important segment in my life.

A Letter from Grace Guthrie

Hi, my name is Grace del Pilar Espinoza Fuentes Hopkins de Guthrie, and I am from Ecuador, South America.

I have lived in the United States for 26 years, and now I reside in Hendersonville, TN with my husband Marty, and two sons Casey and Kenny.

When I was a little girl, I remember my father going to these meetings where he'd volunteer to do service projects with the "important" people from our little town for our community. However, I did not realize that the meetings he attended were Rotary Meetings!

I was proud to tell my friends my father was a Rotarian, because even if I did not understand the whole concept of it, I knew he was a man who cared for people that he dedicated his time and money to the benefit of others.

When I graduated from high school, I came to the United States as an exchange student through the Rotary club. I now feel like I've come full circle by becoming a member myself.

Now that I am a Rotarian, and I have matured, I understand that there is no pride involved. There is something much higher—Service! And service above self! To tell you the truth, when I was invited to Rotary for the first time, I was a little inhibited by just imagining meeting people in important positions in our society. Then, I started to meet people, nice and good people. No titles in front of anyone's name.

I went to Guatemala with a group of them, and I loved this smiling, kind woman who I talked to, sat next to, walked by and had fun with. I just called her "Dianita." Almost to the end of the trip, I heard someone referring to her as "Senator Black." I was astonished! My sweet "Dianita" was a SENATOR!

Then it became real to me. I am part of a special group of people who leave their title out the door and come together with one goal in mind, "...to seek and develop common ground for agreement with people of other lands, going beyond national patriotism resisting any tendency to act in terms of national or racial superiority, preserving the liberty of the individual so that we all may enjoy freedom of thought, speech, and assembly, and freedom from persecution, aggression, want and fear."

Every Wednesday morning I get up early and get excited about sharing with people—just good people who I know have the same dreams of a better world by bringing a message of justice for ALL mankind.

Also I, as everyone else, go through the same doors leaving out my own agenda, my prejudices and pride for exchange of good fellowship, laughs, camaraderie and a wholesome breakfast, seeking more than anything extra hands, stronger voices, united spirits to reach one goal: SERVICE ABOVE SELF!

Is It the Truth? Yes, It Is

A few years ago, I was trying to start my own business. A very good friend of mine, Mike Gaughan, suggested I should really become more involved in the local community to help "spread the word of me." He recommended my first step to be joining Rotary; not just any Rotary club, but the Hendersonville Morning Rotary club. Since Mike only occasionally gives bad advice, I took his recommendation and joined the club.

I had heard from other people that joining a club like Rotary would not pay off in business right away, but you would build relationships and that was more important. I am here to testify to the truth of that statement. As time went by, I had to leave my business and get a real job. I kept my Rotary membership. Not very long ago, I was laid off from that job and am now unemployed. I kept my Rotary membership. This really confounds me since I am a bit of a tightwad. Here I am, unemployed and paying about $500 a year to continue as a member of Rotary. This is nuts; it's crazy. It is the most expensive breakfast in town, but I can't consider abandoning this Rotary membership.

It is all about the people. I have seen people lifted up in this club and let down in this club. They have gone through good times and hard times, life and death situations. The club always reaches out. Not everyone at every time, but enough that a warm feeling of friendship, true concern, and basic human kindness is projected to whomever is in need. At some time, everyone in this club has reached out to another fellow

Rotarian, and made a real difference in that person's life. It's just true.

For me, all of my initial hopes for membership in this club "paying off" in some business way are gone, replaced by a constant amazement at how much of an important element in my life this club has become. I look forward to coming to the meetings. I look forward to hearing the prayer concerns, the happy bucks, the buddy checks, and the speakers (most of the time). When my children were honored as students of the month, they later told me how stunned they were at the atmosphere in the meeting room. They felt comfortable, welcomed, and encouraged to be themselves.

This is a great club, a great organization, with a great purpose. The four-way test is engrained on my mind, and I actually do think of it on occasion, outside the meeting. When I do find work again, I look forward to contributing to many of the causes supported by this club, like Christmas for Kids, Autism, food banks, safe haven groups, and the list goes on. It is a true privilege to be a member here, and I struggle to meet the high ideals.

Don Claussen

My Rotary Odyssey

In October 1984, I was invited to attend a Rotary meeting by Dr. Phillip Head. At the time I really had no idea as to what Rotary was all about. However, as a young professional new to the community I did not think it could hurt to network and meet with other business people in Hendersonville who could help promote my personal business aspirations. During my first few years in the club I did in fact make many acquaintances that proved beneficial to me and the promotion of my practice.

However, as the years passed I became consciously aware that there was more to this fellowship of business men and women than merely self-promotion. I observed the quiet behind-the-scenes selfless contributions of time and money put forth by people I came to respect in an entirely new and inspiring way. I observed the care extended to member families as well as others during times of tragedy and bereavement. I heard the prayers offered in behalf of those in need and for our country.

It has been a unique *opportunity* to be able to pick up trash along the roadway, to serve the under-served in Guatemala, to escort an underprivileged child through Wal-Mart with *Christmas for Kids*, and to be involved in a myriad of other service offerings that Rotary provides. As I reflect back over the past twenty-five years as a Rotarian I realize that my contributions have been minimal compared to with what so many others have done. I only wish I had prioritized my efforts more efficiently.

Rotary has done much more for me than I have for it. For example, Four years ago I underwent a rather serious surgery myself and had the honor and comfort of being remembered by my fellow Rotarians during this trying time. I've met wonderful friends, have had the pleasure of seeing my son inducted as a member, and gotten to study Spanish! I look forward to many more years as a Rotarian. More importantly, I look forward to the unique opportunities for service to others that Rotary affords.

Harold Peeples

A Letter from Nick Peeples

I was first introduced to the Rotary Club when I was in elementary school. My father became a member and left for work early every Wednesday morning wearing his Rotary pin. I remember wondering why he would want to get up so early to go to a meeting that did not have anything to do with his job or with the church that we attended. My father always has been a dedicated family man, professional, and church member. I knew about each of those "organizations" and why he chose to be involved in them, but I did not know much about the Rotary club.

Later, he would ask me if I wanted to go with him from time to time. Most of the time I would find reasons to avoid going. During college, while home on break he asked me to for three weeks straight. I explained to him that I was not really interested in getting up early when I could sleep in with no responsibilities. (Wow, did I have it made!) Finally, the third time he asked me I decided to go with him.

I remember there being a lot of people sitting around eating breakfast and making small talk. I was unimpressed for the most part and thought I might have been better off with the extra sleep! In reality, I had no idea what I was missing and have come to enjoy and look forward to the fellowship I share each week with my fellow Rotarians.

Many years passed from my visit as a college student until the fall of 2008 when I was inducted into the Rotary club.

All the while my father continued his faithful participation in the Hendersonville Wednesday morning group.

As time passed various milestones occurred in my family, some good and some not so good. My sister got married and began to have children; members of the Rotary club were there to congratulate my father on his new grandchildren. I graduated from high school and went off to play football in college; members of the Rotary club were there to celebrate with my father. My father was diagnosed with a brain tumor and spent time in the hospital after surgery and at home recuperating in the weeks following surgery; members of the Rotary club were there to offer their support and send words of encouragement in cards and emails. My grandfather died; members of the Rotary club were present to support my father and our family during our time of loss.

I began to see these people that got up early on Wednesday mornings as people that cared deeply for each other—the relationships that existed between members extended beyond the walls of their weekly meeting room into their everyday lives. Something about that type of friendship attracted me.

In June of 2008 my father asked me to go on the Hendersonville Rotary Club's annual medical mission trip to Guatemala with him. It sounded like a fun trip at the time and I decided to go. It was on that trip that I got to see what the mission of the Rotary Club was about. I was drawn in by the compassion that I saw and by the desire to make the world a better place. It was on that trip that I knew why my dad had chosen to be a part of this organization for so many years. It was also on that trip that I decided that I would also like to be a part of such an organization.

I've been a member now for less than a year. I look forward to the fellowship I share in our meetings and events, and I feel very good about working together with my fellow members to make this world a better place.

I Am a Rotarian Soldier

Rotary allows me to see a different side of many of the well known "movers and shakers" in the community. For example, Robin's tender heart, men such as Lewis Oliver and Jim Fuqua picking up trash along Main Street, the caring heart of Michael Clark and Bill Sinks, the sense of humor of Brenda Payne, Scott Foster, Don and Oliver, the way Julie and Jamie can roll up their sleeves and get a job done (the improbable they can do in their sleep, the impossible may take a couple of minutes). It means seeing community leaders who do not talk about caring for others; they demonstrate it by their actions.

Rotary helps me keep my priorities straight. We are not concerned about a person's economic level. We do not measure a person by their educational degrees. What we are impressed by is a person's willingness to serve others. It is the unselfishness of those who could afford to "buy it done" but would rather roll up their sleeves and do it themselves. Then there are those who, like Peter, do not have silver and gold, but they do have willing hands.

Rotary helps me to realize that it really does not matter who gets the credit as long as the job is done. It is a group that sincerely wants to leave this world a better place than they found it. We know the importance of cooperation. In all the activities I have participated in, it is rare to hear a cross word, but blessings instead. But we also know how to return that enjoyment by making the lives of others more pleasant. I have been preaching since I was 16 (53 years ago). I wish that I could transplant the humility, and generosity, "Service Above Self" attitude of Rotary motto into the church.

Rotary helps me to even better understand the qualities of leadership. Those who lead our club lead by example. It is my goal to become a Paul Harris Fellow. It will take a long time, but by the grace God I will accomplish that goal. I want to accomplish this for the purpose of the fellowship. But I also want to accomplish this because of your example, Bill's example, and the example of others. One day, when they lay me to rest I will have the medallion around my neck. I will wear it into eternity.

When Wednesday rolls around I am ready to get to the meeting. I am not interested in "acclaim" and "fame." I just want to serve. I just want to use my talent as a Christian and as a Rotarian, to make this world a much better place. This club is going a long way in helping me accomplish that goal. When I was inducted into Rotary on June 25, 2008, I stated that the club had inducted a soldier. I am always ready to serve wherever I can because Rotary has entrenched in me that service is the secret to happiness.

Dale C. Flowers

Service: The Heart of Rotary

Service Above Self. It's more than just a slogan for members of the Hendersonville Rotary Club. It's a way of life.

The Club's acts of service have increased as fast as its membership, which doubled in the last ten years. Members represent every walk of life and bring a wide variety of talents to the organization. Each member is called upon to use those talents to the fullest—all in the name of service. Hendersonville Rotary raises more than $45,000 a year through a series of unique and effective fundraising programs. Every dollar raised by the Hendersonville Rotary Club, including money collected at meetings, goes to help others in need. This article offers a glimpse at just a few of the many acts of service performed by the Club in recent years.

One purpose of Rotary Clubs throughout the world is to "provide humanitarian service to those in need." The Hendersonville Rotary Club supports Homebound Meals, The Neighborhood Center and Hendersonville Community Childcare Services, a non-profit childcare facility for working parents who cannot afford private childcare. The Club awards scholarships to Volunteer State Community College and supports the American Cancer Society through Camp Horizon, Habitat for Humanity and many other non-profit projects. Organ Donation and Transplantation Education is also a Club initiative. The Hendersonville Samaritan Center, which recently moved into new facilities, benefits from Rotary support. In 2008 alone, it gave emergency relief to 2,881 Hendersonville families, helped 535 families pay utility bills and assisted 117 families with housing costs. The Community Food Bank, another Rotary beneficiary, provided food to 655 people and provided U.S.D.A. commodities to 206 families– a total of 9.5 tons. The Salvus Center, a faith-based health care provider for the 22,000 working uninsured in Sumner County, was funded in part by the

Hendersonville Rotary. The state-of-the-art Hendersonville Library is a Rotary beneficiary as is the Children are People program and the Imagination Library. The Hendersonville Track, funded in part by Rotary, brings peace, relaxation, and fitness to users.

Children are another key focus for Rotarians. Rotary members serve as mentors, providing guidance, support, and a way for dozens of local elementary school students to share their hopes and dreams. Rotary members work with the local high schools in the Youth Leadership Academy and Youth Exchange, often hosting foreign exchange students in their homes. The Club recognizes outstanding students and teachers at meetings and supports Junior Achievement. Hendersonville Rotary Club members take children Christmas shopping each year in the Christmas for Kids program. Thanks to Rotary, every third grader in Sumner County receives a dictionary and the Wheels in Motion program delivers bicycles to local youth. Rotary Interact, an in-school Rotary Club, sponsors projects to help the community and Rotary's support of the Compass School Partnership gives business leaders a way to support schools.

Every brick laid in Memorial Park in honor of those who keep us safe – service men and women, firefighters and police officers –is an expression of gratitude from the community that honors these heroes. Rotarians work and raise funds to find a cure for cancer in the annual Run for Life. Rotarians are heavily involved in Relay for Life, Sumner County YMCA, Sumner County Adult Education, local school libraries and more. .

Rotary projects like the quarterly Roadside Cleanup are designed to enhance quality of life for all in our community. Members donate a Saturday morning where community leaders, elected officials and many others gather trash on a two-mile stretch of East Main Street.

The Club's heart for service goes beyond city limits, county lines, state borders and national boundaries. With over 80 percent of members active Paul Harris Fellows, the Club is doing its part to help eradicate polio as part of Rotary

International's Polio Plus initiative. The Club's annual medical mission trip to Guatemala is an ongoing outreach to impact the medical needs of some of that region's poorest citizens. Each year between eight and fifteen Hendersonville Rotarians travel to Guatemala, always at their own expense, to participate in this wonderful example of *Service Above Self.*

When disaster strikes, Rotary is there. Hendersonville Rotarians offered much-needed support in the aftermath of hurricane Katrina and after including 2006 tornado outbreak in Sumner County. The Club has been an active participant in Rotary International's Shelter Box Project, which involves assembling boxes containing emergency shelter and provisions for people in areas affected by natural disasters. When the government of Burma turned away foreign aid after a Tsunami, Rotary International was there, bringing Shelter Boxes to people who needed them. In the past few years the Hendersonville Rotary Club has donated over $100,000 in funds, goods and services to those in need.

In the Hendersonville Rotary, no one cares who gets credit for helping others as long as the work is done. *Service Above Self:* this is the heart of Rotary.

Dale Flowers

Money, Money, Money

Making it; giving it: That has been one of the core values and challenges of the Hendersonville morning Rotary Club throughout its forty year existence.

As the Club has grown and matured, so have its fund raising efforts. "We've moved from the community bake sale mentality to the hosting of several mega-signature events each year," said one of the event chairs.

By all accounts, the catalyst for this ramping up of the money gathering was the Memorial Park Fountain, an award winning project that came with a $200,000 price tag.

As Rotary International's Centennial was approaching, every Club was requested to have a community-based project. As the President elect, Todd Odum knew that he needed to start planning ahead to meet the challenge that was to come to fruition during his term of office, 2004-2005.

He said he was driving past Hendersonville's Memorial Park one day and it hit him that significant improvements were needed to the public safety memorial area, especially in the wake of 9/11. There were only a few freestanding small monuments there; those lone columns reallydid not make the visual impact consistent with the honor owed to those fallen heroes.

Odom has a background in architecture and he designed the fountain. His former UT college roommate worked for Hart Freeland Roberts and he did the drawings as a favor to Todd.

From the air, it looks like the Rotary wheel emblem with different colors of concrete. Odum, rightfully proud, says, "It was awarded the outstanding project for the Middle Tennessee district."

He recalls that it was through the efforts of Rotarian Diane Black, then a state representative, that Rotary was eligible to receive $35,000 in matching funds from the state's environmental conservation department. That left $165,000 for Hendersonville Rotarians to raise in little over a year's time.

Approximately $50,000 was generated by the sale of brick pavers. Fortunately, the public was eager to pay to have their names and those they wanted to honor or memorialize imprinted in the brick pavers that surround the fountain. Even with the success of the pavers project, that still left a significant deficit in what was needed.

The Club needed to move beyond the $10,000 profit generating golf tournament and lobster sales and move into the mega-signature events capable of generating $20,000 to $30,000 in profits per event. "Golf tournaments were becoming a dime a dozen and the last year of the lobster sales, the lobsters air-shipped from Maine were dead on arrival," Rae Collier explained.

Festival by the Lake (FBTL), now going into its seventh year, owes its origins to the demands for the "fountain fund." Dave and Diane Black got the idea while traveling in Florida. They attended a successful waterfront seafood festival and thought why not try a similar venue with Hendersonville's lakefront. The idea was presented to the group and it evolved into the successful annual September event that grows in popularity each year.

The logistics of putting on an event of the caliber of FBTL are at best daunting for the most intrepid chair person. Landlocked by the lake and a busy four lane highway, the limited land space of Memorial Park does not lend itself to be an ideal location for large crowd drawing events. Organizers insisted, the festival needed to be on the lake and visible from the Main Street of town, so as the event grew and grew, planning got more and more intricate.

Michael Clark, chairing the event now for the third year in a row, says he got involved first as a volunteer for several years and noted that the event which featured amateur entertainment was usually over by 4 p.m. "I felt like we needed to revamp the venue and build it into a destination event with professional entertainment, an event that had more activities and draw for the public, an event that lasts well into the evening."

The event now features Elvis impersonators, a Wacky Raft Race and a 6 p.m. concert of the Blues Other Brothers Band. The children's activities have been expanded to serve a wider age group with a new sports zone. The vendor list has grown to 100 and the ticket buying public is up to 3,300 by the last count. According to Dennis Greeno, treasurer of the Rotary Foundation, gross sales last year were around $44,000 and expenses at about $23,000. The date for the 2009 event has been set for Saturday, September 19. Clark says he will be praying fervently for no rain on that date.

The other signature event which this April celebrated its fourth year of success is the Days of Wine and Roses annual gala. Co-chaired by Bill Sinks and Brenda Payne, this elegant event features over 200 wines and heavy hors d'oeuvres for guests to sample at the Bluegrass Country Club. This event is patterned after a similar gala in Nashville.

With donated wines from the vendors, a fixed price per guest from the Club and thousands of dollars worth of donated silent auction items, the event usually clears a profit of around $20,000.

Both events go through a rigorous post-event evaluation, so that improvements can be implemented in subsequent years. Clark says he is looking to groom a successor to take over his event.

Both events rely heavily on the talents and enthusiasm of the chairs, co- chairs, and project chairs as well as strong participation by the membership. The Lakeside Rotary Club has joined in to provide assistance as well as the various Interact Clubs from the local schools.

In addition, the Club sponsors a 5K Freedom Run, which is now in its fifth year. Last year's run hit its all time record with 175 runners. That event netted about $4,600 in profits.

Kay Palmer

The Rotary Foundation and Paul Harris Fellows

It would be easy to define the Rotary Foundation as a not-for-profit corporation supported solely by voluntary contributions of Rotarians and friends to advance world understanding, goodwill, peace through the improvement of health, and the support of education and the alleviation of poverty.

But that definition would overlook the 90 years of millions of people and children telling their story about how their lives are better because someone cared.

Founded in 1917, The Rotary Foundation gave its first $500 grant to the International Society for Crippled Children which became the Easter Seals. World eradication of polio is imminent, in large part due to The Rotary Foundation.

The Rotary Foundation gives to other health and education programs annually, whether to fund surgeries for congenital heart defects in India, open heart surgeries in the US for children of the world like 11 year-old Jonathan Olunga from Uganda, even libraries in Viet Nam. Lives are improved through The Rotary Foundation's grants. The Rotary Foundation also funds projects by local and district Clubs. The Hendersonville Rotary received a grant to provide clean water in one village as part of our dental mission to Guatemala. Every dollar given to The Rotary Foundation is invested so that 100 % of the interest is used to help those in need.

Undoubtedly the most important step to promote voluntary giving to The Rotary Foundation occurred in 1957, when the idea of Paul Harris Fellow recognition was first proposed. Although the concept of the making $1,000 gifts to the Foundation was slow in developing, by the early 1970's the program began to gain popularity. The distinctive Paul Harris Fellow medallion, lapel pin and attractive certificate have become highly respected symbols of a substantial financial commitment to The Rotary Foundation by Rotarians and friends around the world. The companion to the Paul Harris Fellow is the Paul Harris Sustaining Member, which is the recognition presented to an individual who has given a contribution of $100, or in whose honor a gift is made, with the stated intention of making additional contributions until $1,000 is reached. At that time the Paul Harris Sustaining Member becomes a Paul Harris Fellow. By 2009, more than 1,160,482 Paul Harris Fellows have made gifts of $1,000 to the Foundation. The distinctive gold pin includes a blue stone to represent each $1,000 contribution up to a total of $5,000 in additional gifts.

The Paul Harris Fellows listed appendix, are committed to making lives and communities better through *Service above Self.*

Rod Lilly

The Kitchen Ladies

Wednesday is a wonderful day, because it always begins well. I'm on the road by 6:40 a.m. and my destination is the morning meeting of the Hendersonville Rotary Club. I get to St. Timothy's Lutheran early, pumped and ready to go. As I enter the building, I remember why I look forward to Wednesdays. As I climb the stairs, the aroma of the greatest breakfast buffet in town surrounds me, and my mouth starts to water.

After exchanging greetings with other Rotarians, it's time to eat, and what a feast awaits us. Two breakfast lines feature dry and hot cereal complete with a variety of fruit for toppings. On the hot food line we can enjoy a multitude of delectable meats, potatoes, fruits, biscuits, gravy, choice of fruit drinks and milk. The feast is always ready by 7:15 a.m. It is breakfast time at Rotary.

What does it take to feed more than 140 Rotary members every Wednesday morning? It takes planning, with work starting days earlier. Some supplies can be ordered in bulk, but the fruits, meats, milk, and other perishables must be purchased each week to insure freshness. It takes a big shopping cart and more than a little driving to get these items at the best price. On Tuesday, preparation begins with slicing, dicing, baking, and planning.

On Wednesday mornings, Karen and Donna are up well before dawn. By 5 AM they are in St. Timothy's kitchen with ten pounds of sausage, nine pounds of bacon, hash browns, biscuits, gravy, oatmeal, grits, eggs, and sometimes pancakes to prepare. They get the huge coffee makers brewing in time for the early risers. They slice the strawberries, cantaloupe, and other fruits and set them out on trays. They cover the eleven rows of tables and set out 157 napkins and coffee cups. Three sets of condiments are put in place for each row of tables.

These morning angels feed, on average, over 140 hungry people in a thirty minute morning rush. They also circulate before the meeting begins to refill coffee cups. It's a big job. To put things in perspective, a restaurant breakfast buffet requires three or four cooks and perhaps four servers, plus a manager and cashier to serve the same number of people in the same amount of time.

Serving is only half the battle. Next comes the clean up. Cereal bowls and utensils must be washed, condiments must be collected and stored. A mountain of table cloths must be laundered. Serving tables must be broken down and stored. The vestibule and fellowship hall must be returned to its original state.

The kitchen ladies make it look easy.

These angels of the morning began this labor of love long before some of Rotarians were born. One Wednesday morning in the late 1970s, Hendersonville Rotary President Wally Nicoll asked his friend, Jane Steinhauer, if she would prepare breakfast for the Club while it was meeting at its then-temporary home at St Timothy's. Jane agreed and it was the beginning of a tradition that is still going strong. At first Jane worked alone. Karen See began helping in 1978, and Donna Cornelius came on board in 1981. Thirty years later, the Hendersonville Rotary Club is still meeting at its "temporary" home and the breakfast tradition started by Jane Steinhauer continues.

As part of the research for this article, I came in early and lent a hand to the kitchen ladies while I watched them work their magic. I learned an important lesson that day. The best way to lend a hand to these morning angels is to stay out of their way!

When I think of *Service Above Self*, I see these wonderful women who start our Rotary day with a warm breakfast. They make a big job look easy and they do it with open hearts, smiles and love!

Dale Flowers

Favorite Rotary Moments

Forty years ago in1969, a few individuals gathered together and the Hendersonville Rotary Club was formed. Their dream was a simple one: to gather weekly for fun and friendship, to support projects that helped make Hendersonville a better place, and above all to serve others. Today, that dream is a reality and that reality is so much more than the dream.

Brenda Moore Payne, President of the Hendersonville Area Chamber of Commerce, joined the club after her husband, Jim Moore, passed away. According to Brenda, "I joined at that time to connect with people from Hendersonville who had been [Jim's] friends and Rotary family. I am grateful they have since become mine."

Friendship is a dominant theme of the Hendersonville Club. Bethany Crain, a Rotarian for 3 years, states simply, "I joined rotary to get involved in the community and meet people. Perception was that Rotary rolled up their sleeves and made a great impact in our area and that is what I wanted, to serve others and make new friends! "

Long-time club member, Bill Taylor, notes the importance of that friendship, "Every meeting we laugh and start the day with a smile. We all have fun at our meetings. We also care a lot about each other by the evidence of how we help each other."

Helping each other is not the goal of Rotary, and it is not the purpose of the Hendersonville Rotary Club. Bill notes that when "Larry Johnson became president, we have evolved from a Club of just pay the dues and fees to one of really working in our community to make it a better place. Larry Johnson started getting us personally involved in participating in our Rotary projects."

The projects are everywhere. The sign at Ellis Middle School proudly includes the Rotary symbol. It also honors the memory of former Rotary Club President, Bob Ellis.

The fountain in Hendersonville's Memorial Park proudly bears the Rotary emblem in tribute to the Rotarians whose work made that fountain a possibility. The Rotary Club's work is not always so visible. It is those invisible projects that make the Rotary experience special

For over 25 years, Bill Taylor has led a mission team to Guatemala. Their mission has been to provide dental and health care to the poor in that country. When he suggested that the Hendersonville Rotary Club join that project, he did not receive excuses, only the question – how can we help? "I am proud to include my fellow Rotarians to make the project bigger and better." Brenda Payne has accompanied Bill to Guatemala on three occasions. "Every time is a blessing."

Not everyone is comfortable going to a foreign country, and that is okay. The Hendersonville Club is proud of the Guatemala mission project, and every member contributes to its mission. Bill, a pediatric dentist, admits that he spends most of his time pulling teeth – not filling cavities. The lack of available dental care makes that a necessity. However, relieving the pain always brings a smile.

Locally, the Hendersonville Rotary Club helps so many. Club members have their favorites. For Bethany Crain, her favorite Rotary projects are the ones that impact the youth. "We have projects such as Interact, RYLA, Youth Merit Awards and Scholarships. They all benefit our youth and invest in the future leaders of our community and world. I have a passion for working with these kids and empowering them to reach their fullest potential." For Brenda Payne, one of these projects provides her favorite Rotary moment. Every month, the Rotary Club donates a bicycle to a student at Gene Brown Elementary nominated by the teachers. Brenda describes the moment, "The first time I visited Gene Brown Elementary to give a bicycle to a student. I do not remember the boy's name but he was so shy, he almost did not come forward , but what a great tribute by the teacher who read his story. Most deserving and I am so glad we started this program."

Some members became Rotarians because their parent were a Rotarian. Some became members because a friend asked them to join. For many, that friend was S.T. Womeldorf, a long-time Rotarian who recently passed away. For S.T., his Rotary legacy is all of the persons who he personally recruited and who will continue working in our community. For all members, the Rotary experience is too much to miss. I just love every Wednesday morning coming in to the room with so many great people who want to help our community. I love the smiles and warmth because I get such a morale boost from being there.

Happy 40th, Hendersonville Rotary Club. Your best is yet to come.

Keith C. Dennen

The Future of Rotary Is In Your Hands

As I prepare to step into my role as President of Hendersonville Rotary for the 2009/10 club year, it seems appropriate that the Rotary International Theme for 2009-2010 is "The Future of Rotary IS IN YOUR HANDS." In our club, we believe that the future of our community is in our hands.

Given our tumultuous times, my goal as president is to encourage our current and future members to not only give or raise monetary funds, but to give "physically" of themselves. Each member will be given the opportunity to match his or her personal and professional talent with the various Hendersonville Rotary Service Projects that are within the four Avenues of Service (Club Service, Vocational Service, Community Service and International Service).

When I joined Rotary nine years ago, I had no idea how much participation in the Club would enrich my life or the joy I would get from helping others. Rotary has given me an opportunity to be involved with great community members, whom I might have otherwise not have known, working together to improve our local community needs through the giving of time and resources, in an environment that is friendly, and compassionate. The more you are involved in Rotary, the more you enjoy it because it is about people who give and people who need. True Rotarians are unique individuals who are "movers and shakers" in their communities. In addition, Rotary provides an opportunity to participate on a global level through Rotary International. Rotary looks beyond its boundaries and joins with its brothers and sisters to improve peace and understanding, while combining resources to tackle significant world problems.

While on vacation three years ago, I had the privilege of visiting fellow Rotarians in Australia and New Zealand. A member of the Rotary Club of Runaway Bay, Australia shared his talent by writing a poem about Rotary. His words capture perfectly what Rotary means to me:

"It is not for the money,
It is not for the fame,
It is not for any person gain,
It is just for the love of fellow man
It is just to lend a helping hand,
It is just to give a little of self,
It is to do something you can't buy with wealth,
It is not medals worn with pride,
It is for the feeling deep inside,
It is the reward down in your heart,
It is the feeling you've been part of helping others far and near,
That makes you a Rotarian."

Garry Krischock
Rotary Club of Runaway Bay Queensland, Australia Club No 23971 District 9640

Robin Williams
President Elect

Thoughts on Rotary

Because of my work, I was acquainted with Rotary. I had worked with Jack Green of Rotary in the mid and late 1990s in regard to the Polio Plus campaign. I knew that Rotary was responsible for major contributions toward the success of efforts of the agency for which I worked (CDC) to eliminate polio from the world. I knew about the motto "Service above Self" and I knew that Rotarians were prominent members of their local communities. I had a great deal of intellectual knowledge about Rotary.

In January of 2006, I became a member of the Hendersonville Morning Rotary Club. Initially, I thought I knew what to expect as a new Rotarian. I would pay dues, attend meetings and learn about those things in which my club was involved. It all seemed rather simple.

At first, I simply observed the process to see how things went. My involvement in the club was minimal, and I learned a few things. I went to most of the weekly meetings and participated in club rituals with other Rotarians.

As time passed, I began to realize that the motto is a not just a phrase, but a way of life for Rotarians. I also am learning that the "four way test" establishes a framework into which all decision-making is placed; not only for Rotary Club activities, but also for other phases of life.

This year, I was given the lead responsibility for a small project for the club. I was to secure and distribute dictionaries to all the County's third grade students. As my team and I brought this to fruition, I was satisfied that I had not let the club down and that my initial involvement was successful. At that moment, I had no idea how wrong my thoughts were.

Shortly after the dictionaries were distributed, I was sent a copy of an e-mail in which a parent had expressed thanks for the gift of the dictionary for her child and praised our club for making it happen. In the end, the club actually received 85 e-mails with similar comments.

When I read the e-mail, I realized that the purpose of the dictionary project was not to test my abilities to produce for the club, but to ensure an act of service for the benefit of someone else. I think I have taken the first step on the road to becoming a rotarian, not just a member of a Rotary Club. My club button has a sticker that identifies me as a "new rotarian". I do not think I'll remove it.

Joe Beaver

A DICTIONARY FOR EVERY CHILD

"The central task of education is to implant a will and facility for learning; it should produce not learned but learning people. The truly human society is a learning society. Where grandparents, parents, and children are students together."
Eric Hoffer

Education lays the foundation for the fulfillment of a person's dreams and aspirations. A dictionary is also one of the tools necessary for helping to lay that foundation. A dictionary is the authority in a child's development of many basic language skills. One of the most significant aspects of being able to use a dictionary is that it helps to develop autonomy and confidence in the learner.

The President of the Hendersonville Rotary Club, Mr. Kim Kim, is from South Korea. He still has the first English dictionary that was given to him as a youngster. It no longer has the front cover and many of the pages are torn. You could say this dictionary has seen better days, but he still cherishes that dictionary and continues to use it. A dictionary is an important part of helping children to learn a language, and that is what it did for Mr. Kim. That was why one of his visions as incoming President of the Club was to provide dictionaries to the children of Sumner County, Tennessee.

Mr. Kim learned about a non-profit organization named "The Dictionary Project," whose primary purpose is to provide dictionaries to third-grade students in the United States. This organization understands that funding for education sometimes cannot provide children with all the things they need and teachers have to spend their own money to provide classroom supplies and reference books. Their goal is to assist organizations that want to participate in its vision by providing mass quantities of dictionaries to these entities.

As President of the Club, Mr. Kim asked the Literacy Committee to undertake this task and bring his vision to fruition. The Committee with the help of the President of the Club raised the funds to ensure the success of this project. A total of 2,109 dictionaries were distributed throughout Sumner County. Enclosed in each dictionary was a letter to the parents explaining that the dictionary was for the child to keep and the importance of a dictionary in a child's life. Also, firmly attached to the inside cover of each dictionary was the "Four Way Test of the Things, We Think, Say or Do," four important principles that each child should follow as they grow and progress in life.

We look ahead in our endeavor with the thought of paying it forward. By giving what we can to our children today, we can ensure that they will be better prepared for tomorrow's leadership roles. It is our hope that one day their dictionaries will be as beloved and well worn as Mr. Kim's. That sums up the purpose of our Club's dictionary project. Our vision is that this project will continue for years to come.

Kent Cochran

BEING A ROTARIAN

Several years ago I moved to a county where I knew very few people. I felt that the best way to network with people from the community was to join an organization that provides services for the community. In my search for an organization to join, one organization that I kept hearing about was Rotary. I found that Rotary is the oldest, most prestigious service club organization in the world. I also found that the main objective of Rotary is service in the community, in the workplace, and throughout the world.

Since becoming a Rotarian I have grown both personally and professionally. Rotary instills in its members leadership, public speaking and communication, organization and planning, and team building. Fellowship was the primary reason Rotary was formed and I experience that very week at Rotary meetings whether attending my club or visiting another club.

The Rotary service that is closest to my heart is literacy. I am very passionate about literacy and when the opportunity permitted itself for me to become a part of the Literacy Committee of the Hendersonville Morning Club I jumped at the chance. The President of the club Kim Kim had a vision to provide every third grade public school student in Sumner County with a dictionary. I along with several others worked to bring his vision to fruition. On the morning we delivered the dictionaries to the club's adopted elementary school everything that encompasses Rotary was evident from the smiles on the faces of those children. That is what it means to be a Rotarian.

A member of the Rotary Club of Fort Collins, Colorado appropriately identified what it means to be Rotarian when he submitted the following to his club:

To Be A Rotarian

To be young is to swim in pools you did not dig;
To be young is to dance to music you did not write;
To be young is to sit under trees you did not plant;
To be young is to seek benefits from a city you did not build;

To be a Rotarian is to dig pools in which you will not swim.
To be a Rotarian is to write music to which you will not dance.
To be a Rotarian is to plant trees under which you will not sit.
To be a Rotarian is to build a city and a community from which you will not benefit.

That is what Rotary is about--**"Maturity."** --Mile High Keyway

Kent Cochran

The Guatemala Project

"The secret of success is constancy to purpose."
Benjamin Disraeli

Sometimes challenges seem too big to tackle. This is especially true when looking around the world and seeing the suffering and poverty so prevalent among third world countries. They often seem impossible to understand much less to solve. It is much safer to tackle the problems in our own backyard, being consoled by the maxim that charity starts at home. But Rotary challenges its members to think big and to devote ourselves to international problems. Easy solutions should not temp us into limiting our vision from seeing international problems that need our involvement. It was, after all, visionary leadership that prompted Rotary to commit themselves to the decade-long program of eradicating the scourge of polio. Understanding that sometimes solutions require "constancy to purpose" over the years, Rotary is to be commended for awarding a district award for the Best Continuation Project.

The Rotary Club of Hendersonville was first made aware of the hopeless plight of children in Guatemala in early 1996. Many of these children have never had access to a dentist or doctor. These represent the poorest of the poor. Since 1996, the Rotary Club of Hendersonville has embraced international service through an annual dental and medical mission to Guatemala. The program was inspired by club member and Pediatric Dentist Dr. Bill Taylor who has led the group each year since the first trip. Club members have partnered with the Rotarians in the Guatemalan Rotary Club, *Las Americas,* to bring dental and medical services to poverty-stricken children. Hendersonville Rotarians are joined in Guatemala with local dentists and a physician who conducts medical screening. Dentists, nurses, dental hygienists, pediatricians, an orthopedic surgeon, optometrists and other health professionals, along with numerous lay assistants from the Club have responded to the desperate needs of the children by working on this project. Each year 8–12 Hendersonville Rotarians travel to Guatemala, always at their own expense, to participate in this humanitarian work. This program exemplifies *Service Above Self*.

In 2005, the mission was expanded to include orthopedic surgery. Tennessee Orthopedic Alliance partner Dr. Wills Oglesby led the surgical team and personally performed over 50 examinations and 15 surgeries resulting in several patients being able to walk again for the first time in years.

For the last several years, the mission efforts have been focused on the Remar Orphanage. This orphanage rescues children born in the slums and/or who exist without family, home, love or education. Many of the impoverished children in this area eek out survival by rummaging for food and other necessities at the municipal trash dump. Over the years, deep friendships have developed with *Las Americas* Rotarians. The orphanage staff and former patients consistently show their gratitude and appreciation by joining in the hard work necessary to provide this much needed care. The ever-present line of children anxiously awaiting the extraction of painful, non-restorable teeth (followed with a hug, a toy and a hygiene kit) is proof of the program's success.

Since the program began, more than 5,000 disadvantaged children and adults who otherwise would not have had access to professional healthcare have received over $700,000 in dental and medical services, in settings as remote as a jungle hut or a newly established hospital. None of it would have been possible without the collaborative efforts of many volunteers here in Middle Tennessee. Rotary mission members say the resulting smiles on the faces of the children make all the time, effort and money worthwhile.

Over the years we have expanded our partnership with the *Las Americas* Club with two new medical projects. Climesa

Hospital treats lower class and poverty-stricken citizens of Guatemala City, and Safe Passage provides medical services and support for those living in and around the city's trash dump. These unfortunate homeless children from the city dump rifle through the discards of the more fortunate for something to eat or wear. Climesa Hospital, Safe Passage and Remar Orphanage each have tremendous needs that the Rotary Club of Hendersonville can help satisfy.

In 2007 the Rotary Club of Hendersonville again expanded its Guatemala medical mission horizon. The Club partnered with the Ophthalmic Department at Volunteer Community College in Gallatin and brought two graduating students, all expenses paid by the Club, to assist in a Guatemalan Eye Clinic Program. These students dispensed prescription eye glasses, some donated and some purchased by the Rotary Club, to needy Guatemalans. This was an outstanding experience for the two young ophthalmic students. Because of this successful ophthalmic program, the club will continue taking Volunteer State Community College ophthalmic students to Guatemala. This is a winning situation for the College, for the students, for our Rotary Club and especially for the Guatemalan people.

The twelve 2007 Rotary mission volunteers that traveled to Guatemala were kept very busy extracting 458 teeth from 260 patients, dispensing 220 eye glasses and health screening 126 medical patients. Hundreds of toys were also given to the children. In addition to pulling teeth, Rotarians cleaned medical and dental instruments, performed blood pressure checks, assembled and delivered free hygiene kits, entertained waiting children with Spanish language posters and Crayons showing proper dental hygiene, and worked with the clinic receptionist to enhance triage for the patients.

Our Rotary mission in 2008 expanded its services by establishing a Dental Clinic, a Pediatric Clinic, an Orthopedic

Clinic, an Ophthalmic Clinic, a Health Screening Clinic, an area for the dispensing of Hygiene Kits, and a toy dispersing area for the children who were treated. All clinics were staffed by professionals, technicians and Rotary volunteers who cared for approximately 700 needy Guatemalans during the week's medical mission.

After more than a dozen years, this Rotary program has developed into a true labor of love. Many Hendersonville Rotarians have traveled to Guatemala repeatedly, working under difficult conditions, with their only desire being to help underprivileged Guatemalans attain better lives.

After the invasion of North Africa by Allied forces in World War II, Sir Winston Churchill was asked if this invasion marked the beginning of the end for Nazi domination. He answered that this success wasn't the beginning of the end but the end of the beginning. Our club realizes that each year we make a difference in the lives of Guatemalan children but that we have only scratched the surface and that we are truly at the end of the beginning in our international humanitarian project in Guatemala.

Pat Lebkuecher

A MIRACLE IN GUATEMALA
By: Tim Lynch, D.Min., PhD, Diplomat, Energy Psychology
ACEP

On June 2, 2012, a small twin-engine Cessna piloted by Dr. Bill Taylor, carrying four passengers and a planeload of donated medical supplies landed in Guatemala. About the same time, an American Airlines plane carrying the remaining 12 Rotary Club volunteers to work for a week at Remar Orphanage also landed in Guatemala. This is the yearly destination for the Hendersonville Rotary Club's annual medical, dental, and optical missionary team. Most of us were anxious visiting Central America for the first time with its civil strife, severe political rivalry, dictatorships, drug cartel surrounding the city, and significant government unrest. This has been a country of corrupt politicians with tremendous wealth with the remainder of the population generally quite poor. The average income is around $900 (USD) year.

We were warned that the most dangerous thing you could do was to use your cell phone in public, as it was likely you would be robbed and possibly killed as your cell phone was stolen. As I considered the potential danger, I recalled the initial invitation to accompany my son, Tim, who was this year's leader of the Rotary project begun by a dentist in our club 16 years prior. I found it hard to say no to my son who is a very sincere and articulate young man. He is a natural motivator who is, not surprisingly, one of the top salesmen in his medical equipment supplies company. All of these supplies had been donated to the Guatemalan mission by his generous customers.

We were so fortunate to be met at the airport by the Guatemalan Rotary Club who provided our transportation and communication needs for us throughout the entire mission trip. What a wonderful group of caring people!

The medical team this year included physicians, dentists, ophthalmology students & staff, and for the first time included a clinical psychologist, me. Initially, I was assigned to the dental team to assist in whatever way I could to reduce stress and assist in pain management, including being the amateur magician to distract children from the scary medical and dental procedures. I really enjoyed this role assisting; however, within a couple of hours it became increasingly apparent to me that there was a much greater need for my clinical services as a trauma therapist because there were so many individuals suffering from severe emotional trauma.

These traumas clearly met the criteria for posttraumatic stress disorder, PTSD, as described in the Diagnostic and Statistical Manual of the American Psychiatric Association. With typical examples such as having witnessed their parents killed, experienced violent crime, had been raped or traumatized, I decided to utilize some of my training in the advanced techniques from energy psychology.

Although my doctoral training at both Vanderbilt and Union University was fairly traditional from an academic perspective, I am a lifelong learner and have never stopped trying to learn every meaningful and powerful treatment that enhances behavior change and reduces human suffering. The first area outside of my doctoral studies which brought about significant behavior change within me was my training from the American and International Society of Clinical Hypnosis, and over the years I received their highest level of training. Their founder, Milton Erickson, M.D., considered the father of modern hypnotherapy was my true role model!

The next two years I trained in NLP, Neurolinguistic Programming, and was certified as both a Practitioner and a Master Practitioner by the originators, Bandler and Grinder. This opened up another fascinating world to quickly assist troubled people with provocative changes. I also studied directly with Victor Frankel, M.D., author of the world famous and bestselling, "Man's Search for Meaning", and received training from him on three occasions. There were several other mentors over the years that encouraged me to develop the use of psychotherapy approaches that helped me to learn to quickly focus on addressing the immediate needs of people who were experiencing specific and often significant suffering in their lives.

About 12 years ago I feel very fortunate to be introduced to the field of energy psychology by my longtime friend and colleague psychologist J.B. Fournier. J.B. and I have been avid learners and friends since the 1970s. The field of Energy Psychology is a new and dramatically different treatment approach that can rapidly reduce and eliminate traumas; in fact the results are so incredibly fast and powerful that the American Psychological Association and the vast majority of psychologists are reluctant to use it. Sometimes called 'acupuncture without needles', the ideas underlying energy psychology have been around for thousands of years as a pre-dimension of quantum physics, eastern medicine, and various energetic patterns and systems, such as meridians and chakras. It has successfully been used for many years to reduce or eliminate negative reactions to trauma, anxiety and fearful situations, to name a few. In ways that we do not fully understand, energy psychology quickly assesses unconscious patterns and beliefs as well as their corresponding resistances, releasing these limiting beliefs and freeing negative emotional states, and replacing them with positive, energetic states of mind. No doubt this emerging school of psychological intervention, energy psychology, will continue to gain increased acceptance as a vibrant therapy to effectively treat traumas and other challenging human problems.

By mid-morning of the first day as a dental assistant, it became apparent to me and others that the traumas of our patients were so clearly manifest that I was asked to offer my skills, training, and passion to assist these deeply troubled individuals. I established a makeshift office and was greatly assisted with the expert services of one of the five translators. These superb translators were high school graduates, and family members of our fellow Guatemalan Rotary Club. Each day I had a different translator due to their excitement of being a part of the sessions of trauma treatment. The translators told me they could not believe the change in each person before the session compared to after the session. I had also trained each of the translators in the tapping sequences to prepare them for the trauma they would experience themselves by listening to the patients in order to translate their stories. It was not long before there was a waiting line that remained steady throughout the entire week.

My conceptual framework was as follows: the situation we're in is somewhat similar to a M*A*S*H unit, with the majority of people currently experiencing tremendous crisis. As we know, crisis is an oriental word, which essentially means "dangerous opportunity", and for the vast majority of people that I would see, this would be their only opportunity to receive a mental health intervention. Secondly, I strongly felt a sense of rapport with them. The medical group, led by Dr. Taylor, had been coming to this facility for over 20 years, providing a variety of health services, and the community had a great confidence in the Rotary Club and their 16 years of service in promoting overall health. Thirdly, my goal with each patient is to address their issues (about 60% had traumas), and facilitate the healing process. The ages of the patients throughout the week ranged from age 6 to 75 and several were residents of the orphanage (240 residents) where the temporary clinic was set up.

The presence of immediate and trusting rapport was evident from my first consultation and all the way to the very last consultation at the end of the week. I realized, as did the patient, that this was a one-time intervention. I felt very confident that I could connect with each person and help them address, in an effective way, the resolution of their problem. As I sat facing each patient I sat as close as possible because in the Latin culture closeness further instills a sense of trust and a spirit of helpfulness. After a relatively brief interview in which the problem (s) were identified, I also obtained a measurement of their "subjective units of distress", often referred to as SUDS. The scale goes from 0 to 10, with 10 marking the highest level of trauma. Unfortunately, 90% of the trauma patients identified their initial level at "10" as we began our session.

I generally began each treatment with the energy psychology modality EFT: a tapping sequence of the 11 meridians and several acupuncture points. This immediately begins to release the emotional and psychological traumatic distress, as well as connecting many to their spiritual self. For those with very intense trauma, the tapping was preceded by EMDR, Eye Movement Desensitization and Reprocessing, a technique that amazingly changes the neurochemistry and subsequently the mood and behavior associated with this trauma. I continued my intervention by utilizing all the skills that were appropriate, which I have developed over the years, including NLP, BSFF and several others, which help to stretch the patient to a positive futuristic state of mind, leaving behind the trauma. I often would utilize a technique in which the patient would sort of 'pull out of their body' any remnants of the trauma by a sweeping move motion down the body, wiping off their arms and hands, leaving IT, THE TRAUMA, on the floor, or waving it behind them, metaphorically speaking… placing it in the past. At this point I would check their SUDS reading and it was often at three or four. We would continue to process the trauma and by the end of the session about 90% would say, with a sigh of relief and a pleasant smile on their face, their SUDS was at zero! No doubt future mission trips will include pre and post PTSD testing to facilitate research, development, and training.

Initially, the majority of the patients were stuck in a negative loop in which they would neurolinguisticly feel "stuck" in the auditory state with their eyes down and to the left and then "looping" to the right with a downward glance (feeling the traumatic state down to the right), often called "downright disgusting." Often, a new sense of freedom would be experienced by the patient assisting them to move into an all positive visual state in which they would, in the neurolinguistic context, be looking upward and into the future. This process was picked up very quickly by all of the patients as they were trained several times until they showed some proficiency in this process of being in charge of their own mental health treatment. Incorporated throughout this process was a specific breathing pattern: breathing in fairly deeply through the nose and exhaling through the lips. I would assist them, often subconsciously, to match my breathing which would further develop and maintain rapport with each other. As the patient would arrive at this new founded state of calmness, hopefulness and peace, I would ask them to place their hand on their heart as the anchor (BSFF) to an altered state of consciousness. Then I would usually place my hand on their hands firmly reinforcing this state, as I would say, "This peace will always be in your heart, when you feel fear, trauma, or other negative thoughts, place your hand on your heart to remind you forever of this peace that you now possess."

Throughout this entire process, the patient and I maintained very close eye contact. As I listened to the intensity, the violence, and the tragedy, I would occasionally have tears in my eyes as the patients arrived at a cathartic point where weeping and sometimes moaning were present as they initially processed their trauma. My eyes, my body language, my concern, my respect, and my caring helped them to find hope and confidence in love. With each patient there was an intense practice of the tapping, BSFF and other energy psychology techniques, along with the breathing techniques and positive neurolinguistic "reprogramming".

Never in my career have I seen so many people with so many traumas in such an intense environment as I did in this remote village and orphanage in a very desperate place in the outskirts of Guatemala. My professional goal was to provide the most intense psychological help in a limited time, very much as I would in any crisis or emergency intervention that I have had scattered through my practice of 35 years as a therapist. But I never imagined that I or any clinical psychologist or therapist of any kind could get the almost miraculous results that we achieved so rapidly on this humanitarian mission. We were all blessed.

No doubt, as a team, we gave a lot as our hometown Rotary Club joined with the Rotary Club of Guatemala, sharing the motto: 'SERVICE ABOVE SELF'. I suspect that each of us received a lot more, in so many wonderful ways, than we actually gave, though we gave our best to our fellow man. Next year's mission trip will be a must for all of us.

In the spirit of the Harrison Keeler mantra, "Do good work… stay in touch" and please join us at the next Rotary Club medical, dental, optical, and psychological mission!

A Visit to the Garbage Dump
By Tim Lynch, Ph.D, DCEP

Early one Sunday morning a Rotary club mission group embarked to the Remar Orphanage in a remote village in the outskirts of Guatemala. On the way to the medical side our Rotary club guide, Carlos had the bus driver stop at the community cemetery for us to see the aboveground catacombs (some three stories high), which have been there for hundreds of years. What an incredible site with locks and families visiting their loved ones, often climbing tall ladders to affix a flower or picture on top of the catacomb.

We were about ready to leave the cemetery to head to our work of preparing the clinic for weeklong medical service for hundreds of people who would become our patients, when Carlos said, "follow me. I want to show you something." But I have to warn you, this will be disturbing! We cautiously followed Carlos toward the edge of the cemetery that was built upon a bluff overlooking the valley. From the distance there appeared to be a beautiful view, however, as we got closer to the edge of the bluff, the stench was awful. I have a fairly strong constitution and stomach, however, I felt close to vomiting, especially worsened as I looked over the bluff into the largest garbage dump (several acres) I have ever seen. What was most disturbing was in the middle and throughout this dumb were tiny tents were families live. ... Their whole life! Many were born in the dump, live their life in the dump, and died there! This is truly a most overwhelming size and experience for all of us. How is it possible that fellow human beings could live in such a desperate and despicable way? As we gathered back on our bus heading toward the orphanage, there was dead silence, as all of us attempted to process what we had just experienced. Wedded not really talk about it, we just attempted to "process it." It was not long before we arrived at our destination, and we became quickly engrossed in our preparation for our busy clinic week experience. We have the cemetery just seemed to fade away, but it reallydid not.

When Saturday morning arrived, following an incredibly busy week of providing medical, dental, optical, and psychological treatment to over 1,600 people we were exhausted, but so fulfilled with the services we shared. Some of us spend the morning on a zip line going across the coffee bean plantation. This was truly an exhilarating experience. We had gathered for lunch on top of a magnificent mountain adjacent to the Guatemala volcano. I cannot remember ever being in such a pleasant beautiful restaurant on top of the mountain overlooking the majestic town of Antiqua, Central America. We're just a few miles from Guatemala. I was fortunate to be sitting next to a very pleasant Rotarian leader Carlos and I have to ask him, "the burning question." How was it possible that the community of Guatemala could allow so many people to live in the garbage dump adjacent to the cemetery? Carlos smiled at me and said, "Tim, let me help you out. Several years ago there was a humanitarian effort, he was part of it, that went down into the dump and invited everyone to come out with a promise. "We will take care of you, we will give you housing, we will clean you up, we will reprogram you, we will give you an education, and if you cooperate with us. We will give you jobs, even the most prestigious job as a waiter or waitress at this magnificent restaurant in Antiqua. Wow! What an opportunity! I said to Carlos, what happened? Well, to our surprise, only about 25 or 30 took the offer and unfortunately the majority elected to stay in the end, that's where they are today. I was stunned. I was speechless, just for a moment. Well, Carlos what happened to the 25 to 30 who chose to come out of the dump, where are they, what their story? Carlos chuckled, and said remember, we promise to give them a wonderful job at the most prestigious restaurants in our community. We are sitting in this prestigious restaurants and every one of the waiters and waitresses had been born in the garbage dump!

I am sure every reader who is reading this story. At this point in time in their life would readily say, "good grief, how could they stay in that dump... I never would do that; I would've gotten right out!"

No doubt this story is not only true but it is a metaphor for each of us in life. Why do we stay "in our garbage dump?" When we really have the opportunity to exit? What keeps us in the dump? How magnificent would our lives become? If you decide to step out... just like the 25 or 30 Guatemalans!

Rotarians Make Dreams Real

As we all know, Paul Harris and three of his friends began Rotary in 1905 in Chicago. In 1947, Paul died and in 1957 it was decided that when $1,000 was contributed to the Rotary Foundation in a person's name, that person would be recognized as a Paul Harris Fellow. This honors Paul Harris as well as pays tribute to the contributor. Working to achieve this recognition has increased contributions by Rotarians. Reading about and understanding the outstanding things that are done with this money should prompt all of us to become a Paul Harris Fellow. Eradication of polio, humanitarian grant projects for such things as clean water, ambassadorial, cultural, peace and teacher scholarships are some of the thing this money does. Only half of what we give in any given year comes back to our district in 3 years to be administered by us (it was over $160,000 in 2007-2008).

I have written these things to encourage you as a member of this club to work towards becoming a Paul Harris Fellow. Kim Kim tells me that he has a goal for this club to be 100% Paul Harris Fellows while he is president. This is certainly a challenge but I believe that you can do it. Other clubs in our district have done it, Clarksville Sunrise being the most recent. I encourage you to begin now working with Kim on this goal. Just think what an accomplishment it will be and the vast amount of good that will be done with the money. Remember that "Rotary Shares" and Rotarians "Make Dreams Real."

Rufus Clifford M.D.

District Governor 6760, 2007-2008

Dong Kurn Lee, President   January 2, 2009
Rotary International
One Rotary Center
1560 Sherman Ave.
Evanston, IL 60201-3698

Dear President Lee,

Greetings from the Hendersonville Morning Rotary Club. My name is Miss Robin Williams and I am President Elect serving under our dedicated leader President Kihyon Kim (we refer to him as Kim Kim). Kim is the greatest example of a true Rotarian who leads by example.

Our Rotary Club is located in beautiful Hendersonville, Tennessee, USA and we are proud to be part of Rotary International serving in District 6760. Hendersonville Morning Rotary Club came into existence in 1969 and we currently have more than 160 members. Your theme "Make Dreams Real" means more to Hendersonville Morning Club than you may know. Throughout these 39 years, our Rotarians have participated in programs that support your mission and vision for children. Here are a few examples of how we are Making Dreams Real:

- Guatemala Medical Mission Trip - Since the program began, more than 5,000 disadvantaged children and adults who otherwise would not have had access to professional healthcare have received over $700,000 in dental and medical services, in settings as remote as a jungle hut or a newly established hospital.

- Community Child Care Center (CCC) –The club makes a regular donation of $250 per month to CCC. We also make additional donations that are estimated at $5000 per year. In December 2008, we sent a special donation of $500.

- Wheels in Motion – Two bikes are given each month to needy children during the school session. Costs are about $135 for each bike and helmet. In addition, Rotary Members mentor and tutor children at schools where the population of students are from low income families.

- Christmas for Kids – 600 needy children get about $275 to shop for their families and themselves. Money is raised by local donations and by a major Country Music concert.

- Youth Exchange Students – Rotarians house and feed students yearly

- Ambassador Scholarship – Last year, we had the opportunity to assist in a special fundraising project assisting Doran Lee and family. Doran was here on a scholarship from Seoul, Korea. Unfortunately, she was involved in a car accident. Doran was transported from the scene after sustaining major head injury and face lacerations. She received trauma care, several surgeries and follow-up care. Working with our district, we raised $10,000 to help with her medical care and needs.

Personally, I had the privilege of teaching English in South Korea from 1991 to 1994 where I taught University students in Jeonju for a year and spent another year in Seoul teaching physicians and business professionals. What an incredible experience this was for me. I will never forget my dear students and treasured Korean friends. I have such a love and appreciation for the Korean people and their culture. I believe this is one reason why Kim Kim and I became instant friends when we met as fellow Rotarians and walked hours for the Rotary's Relay for Life.

This year, "Make Dreams Real" has already become a reality for Kim. Kim Kim is the first and only Korean American President in the USA. Kim was just nominated to be our Districts Assistant Governor for 2009. Kim's dream includes tearing down barriers in our society. In Rotary, we are one family, and he hopes we as Rotarians can help change divided society as one.

I remember Kim Kim telling us that he had the privilege of meeting with you and your lovely wife while you visited Nashville in March for the Multi District PETS. Under Kim's leadership, we are striving to become a 100% Paul Harris Membership Club. (Kim Kim is a Paul Harris Fellow and Major Donor). In addition, the Hendersonville Morning Rotary Club will be celebrating our 40th year Anniversary on June 19, 2009. It would be such an honor to have you at the banquet. However, we understand that the convention in England is during the same time. So if there is another time that would fit your schedule, I would be honored to coordinate your visit.

President Lee, it would Make Dreams Real for the Hendersonville Rotary Morning Club if you were able to join us as an honorary guest representing the Rotary International and our Korean brothers and sisters. Your airfare, room and board accommodations would be provided by member donations.

Thank you for your sincere consideration.

Kind Regards,

Robin C. Williams

친애하는 RI President 이동건 회장님께

바쁘신 중에도 PETS (President Elect Training Seminar)을 위해 내쉬빌에 오신 것을 진심으로 환영합니다. 이회장님께서 Rotary International 회장으로 내정되셨다는 발표를 접한 후 꼭 한번 뵙게 될 수 있었으면 하는 것이 제 소망이었는데 제가 살고있는 내쉬빌에 이렇게 직접 와주셨으니 어찌나 감사하고 기쁜지 모르겠습니다.

열일곱 살 때 고국을 떠나 온가족이 이곳 미국 내쉬빌지역에 정착한지 어느덧 28년이 되었습니다. 백인사회인 미국에서 한국인이기 때문에 갖은 수난과 어려움을 겪고 있습니다만 그래도 감사하고 굳굳이 일어설수 있었던 것은 바로, 아이러니하게도 한국인이라는 자부심과 긍지때문입니다. 특히 로타리 창설이래 이동건 회장님께서 한국인으로서는 사상처음으로 Rotary International 를 이끄시게 되었다는 것은 한 개인만의 영광이 아니라 온 한국인과 로터리를 사랑하는 세계인의 자랑이며 영광이 아닐수 없습니다. 다시 한번 축하와 감사를 드립니다.

이회장님,

제가 가입되어있는 The Rotary Club of Hendersonville 은 155명 이 백인으로 구성되어 있습니다. 이런 환경에서 내세울 것 하나 없는 저를 이회장님 임기인 같은 해에 저를 클럽회장으로 뽑아준 회원 모두에게 그저 감사하고 최선을 다해 섬기겠다는 말밖에는 할 수가 없습니다. 제가 2년 전에 클럽회장으로 내정되었을 때 반대와 불가능하다는 생각들을 무릅쓰고 다짐한 것이 있습니다. 제가 매달 회원모두에게 부치는

편지를 읽으시면 전 내용을 아시겠지만 회원 155 명 모두 (100% Paul Harris Fellow Club) PHF Club 이 되는 것입니다. 도산 안창호 선생께서 꺼지지 않는 불씨라는 제목으로 이런 말씀을 하셨습니다. "죽지 않으면 산다. 뜻이 있으면 펼쳐야 한다. 믿음이 있다면 굽힐 수는 없는 일이다. 너에게 참이 있느냐? 있다면 두려워할 게 없다. 너에게 힘이 있느냐? 없다면 길러야 한다." 저는 이 목표를 위해 전 노력을 다할 것이며 이회장님 임기 때에 반드시 달성하고 싶습니다. 2009 년 6 월 16 일이면 저의 클럽 창설 40 주년 이기도 하니 절호의 기회라 여겨집니다.

그리고 이회장님께서는 동안양 클럽회원이신 이규철 선생님과 서울 고등학교 선후배로 알고 있습니다. 이화여자대학교에 다니던 이 도란 이라는 학생이 이곳 내쉬빌에 6 개월간 Cultural Ambassadorial Scholarship 으로 공부하러 왔다가 지난달 2 월 29 일 날 고국으로 돌아갔는데, 이규철선생님이 작은 할아버님 되신다고 하더군요. 도란이 학생이 뇌와 얼굴에 치명적인 교통사고를 당한 후 삼 일간의 의식불명에서 기적적으로 살아나 고국으로 돌아갈 수 있었던 것은 물심양면으로 도와주고 기도해 준 로터리 클럽회원 때문입니다. 도와준 모든 회원들에게 보답하는 길은 제가 세운 100% PHF Club 을 달성해 도란이 같은 학생들에게 더 많은 장학기회를 제공하는 것이며, 소아마비를 세계적으로 전멸시키는 것이며, 어렵고 불쌍한 전세계 어린이들에게 지금보다 더 나은 환경을 만들어주어 가난과 굶주림으로부터 벗어나게 해주는 것이라고 믿습니다. 그래서 회장님의 RI Theme 인 Make Dreams Real 이 각 어린이들 마음속에 자라 마음껏 꿈을 펼칠 수 있도록 그런 환경을 만들어 주는 것이 우리 모두의 책임이며 사명이라고 생각합니다.

바쁘신 이회장님께 이처럼 어려운 부탁을 드려 죄송합니다만 The Rotary Club of Hendersonville 회원들에게

100% PHF Club 을 달성하기 위해 격려와 용기의 편지를 써
주셨으면 하는 것입니다. 저의 클럽이 40 년 전인 1969 에 창설된
후 2000 년이 되어서야 처음으로 한국인을 회원으로 받아들였고,
올해 최고의 로타인으로 2003 년도에 뽑아주었고, 그리고
이제는 한국인을 회장으로 선출해준 저의 회원 모두에게 꼭 PHF
Members 가 될 수 있도록 편지를 써주시면 저 개인의 영광일
뿐만 아니라 저의 클럽회원 모두에게 크나큰 영광이 될 것입니다.

그리고 저의 클럽의 성공담이 입으로 입으로 전해져서
다른 클럽에까지 번진다면, 그래서 온 세계 로터리클럽이 그 해
목표로 삼아 정진해 준다면 한국의 옛말처럼 세세 송송-큰 나는
죽어도 작은 나는 살아 이루어질 때까지 몇 번이든 환생한다는-
이 될 것입니다. 올해는 어제보다 더 나은 해가 될 것이며, 내일
우리는 아무리 어려운 일이 닥쳐도 소아마비를 전멸시키듯
한마음으로 뭉친 1.2 million Rotarians 에게 이루지 못할 것이
없다고 생각됩니다. 비석에 자기 이름 석자 남기기 위해 자신에
투자하는 사람보다 모든 로터리회원들이 자아봉사, "Service
Above Self" the Rotary motto 처럼 남을 위해 살다 보면 지나는
사람들의 마음속에 비석이 되어 영원토록 남아있으리라
믿어집니다.

저와 클럽회원이 쓴 편지를 선물로 드리오니 즐겁게
읽어주십시오. 그리고 다시 한번 내쉬빌에 오신 것을 진심으로
환영하며 짧은 시간이나마 회장님과 사모님을 뵙고 모시게 된
것에 감사 드립니다. 제가 도울 일이 있다면 무엇이든 꼭
알려주십시오. 미국사회에서 Korean-American 들이 피부색
때문에 부당한 대우나 공정히 주어져야 할 기회마저 갖지 못하는
것은 앞 세대가 밑거름 되기를 거부하고 한갓 눈의 욕망과 자기
가족만이라는 좁은 테두리 안에서 벗어나지 못하기 때문이라는
것이 저의 소견입니다. 맞닿은 옆집에 불이 났는데도 나와는
전혀 상관없는 일이라며 도와주기는커녕 가만히 지켜만 본다면

결국 자신뿐만 아니라 이웃과 함께 온 가족이 피해를 입는 것은 당연한 이치입니다. 자기 가족이 중할수록 남 또한 중요하며 남 없이는 나 또한 존재하지 않는다는 생각, 그래서 피부가 다르고, 언어가 다르고, 풍습이 다르더라도 미국 속 한국인은 일꾼이 되어 앞장서서 미국사회와 세계 속에 뛰어들어야 된다고 생각합니다.

모든 사람이 태어났지만 모든 사람이 다 사는 것은 아닌 것처럼, 죽어야만 하는 우리인생, 한번밖에 주어지지 않은 삶이기에 회장님처럼 맘껏 남을 위해 살다 가렵니다. 감히 회장님같이 덕이 높으신 분에게 이런 못난 글을 올린다는 것이 잘못인 줄 알면서 회장님에 관한 글을 로터리잡지책에서 접한 후 많은 감동을 받아 저도 모르게 이런 글을 드리게 되었습니다. 부디 용서하십시오. 저의 짧은 소견을 이해해 주시고 많은 조언과 충고를 기대하겠습니다. 아무쪼록 건강하시고 저의 글을 읽어 주셔서 감사 드리며 다음 기회에 또 뵐 수 있기를 고대하겠습니다. 함석헌옹의 "뜻으로 본 한국역사"에 제가 인생의 지침대로 삼는 글이 담겨있습니다. 같이 나누며 그만 줄일까 합니다. 안녕히 계십시오.

낮은 일은 높은 마음이 아니고는 할 수없고, 작은 일은 큰 마음이 아니고는 할수없고, 더러운 것을 치우려면 무엇으로도 더러워지지 않는 마음이 있어야하고, 죄를 처분하려면 어떤 죄라도 상하지 않는 거룩한 혼이 있어야 할 것이다. 이것을 하기 위하여 하나님이 우리에게 주신 것이 "착함"이다. 불인지심이다. "인"이다.

김기현 2008 년 3 월 26 일

Dear Mr. R.I. President,

How are you, R.I. President D.K. Lee? I'm Doran Lee, a recipient of the Cultural Ambassadorial Scholarship from Korea Rotary District 3750. First of all, I'd like to congratulate you for being the first Korean R.I. President. The reason why I am writing you this letter is to thank you for the precious relationships and opportunities given to me by Rotary.

I am currently enrolled in Ewha Women University, majoring in English literature as a junior; I lived in the U.S. beginning last July for six months as a Rotary scholar. Rotary provided me, who was lacking of many qualities, an essential experience in my life, and let me associate with many wonderful people.

While I was attending English Language School in Nashville, Tennessee for six months, I experienced the real American life and visited many Rotary Clubs to speak about Korea and share my personal experience with members. Coincidentally, I was very happy to hear that you are visiting Nashville this week. Also, when I was in the U.S., my host family was Rotarian Kim Kim—the member of Hendersonville Rotary Club; I was told he would assist you for a few days while you are in Nashville.

I heard that it is very difficult to meet Korean Rotarians in the U.S.; at the same time, Mr. Kim Kim, whom I have met, is like my family benefactor in the smaller city of Nashville. Nashville is a small but sentimental city, and many kind and good people live there. However, I was afraid and a stranger at first, living in a strange land for six months by myself as an international student.

I met my host and counselor Rotarian Kim Kim and his family during that time, and they welcomed me into their home and warmly took care of me better than my own family would. The reason why I am so grateful, more than anything, to Mr. Kim Kim and all Rotary Clubs in that district is that I received so much help from them when I had a serious automobile accident last November on Thanksgiving night. My friend was driving negligently while I was sleeping in the back seat of the car on the Interstate. I had several surgeries at the Vanderbilt Medical Center in Nashville, and I was standing in the middle of life and death.

My parents flew in from Korea several days later, but Mr. Kim Kim and many other Rotarians took great care of me, while I was unconscious and had no family at the time. When I was in and out of a coma, Mr. Kim Kim, whose job was only as a counselor for me, ran toward me first and tried to take care of everything that was happening. After I was discharged from the hospital, my mom and I moved in with Mr. Kim Kim's family for three months, and they treated us with warmth and comfort. Also, many Rotary Clubs and Rotarians centered around the Hendersonville Rotary Club not only prayed for me and visited me in the hospital but also raised money to pay enormous hospital bills and comforted me in all sincerity.

Although the automobile accident was a huge ordeal and a crisis in my life, it made me realize many important things and receive love through the friendship that Rotary made for me. Thankfully I am fully recovered and have safely returned to Korea.

Rotary is a huge opportunity, fellowship, and love to me. Therefore, I sincerely appreciate and congratulate you for R.I.

Korean President as well as for representing such a wonderful Rotary.

I truly wish you, too, have a meaningful and enjoyable time in Nashville, where it meant so much to me. I conclude my letter saying have a good day.

Truly Yours,

Doran Lee, a recipient of the Cultural Ambassadorial Scholarship

도란 이에게,

안녕! 안녕이라는 말이 서먹하게 들리는구나. 도란이가 아직도 곁에 있는 것 같아 네가 지냈던 방을 두리번거리게 된다. 그리고 너와 부모님이 남기고 간 종이조각 하나라도 간직하고 싶은 마음이다. 같이 나눈 시간들이 그리워 아줌마와 나는 너와 부모님에 관한 이야기 꽃을 피우며 웃지만 그래도 보고 싶은 사람을 볼 수 없다는 것은 큰 아픔이 아닐 수 없다. 아람이가 내년에 유럽으로 일년간 공부하러 가면 내 딸이 무척 보고 싶어, 나 어떻게 하지? 아버님, 어머님, 그리고 세란이도 잘 계시지? 세란이만 보지 못해 어떻게 생겼는지 궁금하다. 무척 예쁘고, 귀엽고, 착한 동생일 거야. 언젠가 볼 날이 있을 거야.

도란아, 공항에서 너를 어떻게 보내나 하고 도란이가 떠나기 전날 많이 걱정했단다. 병원에 있었을 때는 네가 혼수상태여서 아저씨가 맘껏 울어도 보는 사람이 없고 설사 있었어도 너 아버지 되는 사람인줄로 착각해 괜찮았는데 떠나는 너에게 웃는 모습으로 보내주고 싶은데, 과연 그렇게 할 수 있을까 걱정이 되었거든. 다행히 도란이 친구가 와줘 쉽게 도망칠 수 있었지……

이제는 만남의 순간보다 헤어짐에 더 가슴이 설렌다. 이렇게 도란이와 좋은 사람들을 떠나 보내고 남은 자리에서 헤어짐의 슬픔을 겸허히 받아들일 수 있고 또 웃음을 지을 수 있었던 것은 꼭 만남이 있을 거라는 전제에서겠지. 짧은 만남의 설렘은 기쁨보다 슬픔에 더욱 가깝다. 언제가 보내줘야 하니까! 너 때문에 너무나 좋은 사람들을 많이 만났고, 그래서 많은 사람과 헤어져야 했지만 그 짧은 시간 동안 너무나 행복했고

고마웠다. 너 아니었으면 나와 우리가정 어떻게 이런 아름다운 추억을 가질 수 있었을까? 그리고 한국 하면 의무적으로 남겨진 먼 친척밖에는 생각나는 것이 없었는데 이제 나와 아줌마에게는 새로운 땅을 찾은 것처럼 한국이 그리워졌다. 너와 세란이, 그리고 부모님이 계시는 한국이 보고 싶고, 가고 싶고, 두고두고 마음속에 간직하고 픈 그런 곳으로 되어버렸다.

이곳 내쉬빌신문에 도란이 사진이 나와 부친다. Vena Stewart Elementary School 에 다니는 학생 모두가 너 때문에 꿈을 가지게 되었고 우리 로터리회원이 할 수 없었던 일들을 대신 해줘 무척 고맙다. 물질적으로는 작은 선물이 될련지 모르지만 너의 선행이 그들 모두에게는 가장 아름답고 귀중한 선물이 되었다. 그리고 이틀 동안 로터리 인터내셔널 회장님 내외분과 좋은 인연을 맺게 해준 것에 고맙고 도란이 할아버님께 내가 감사해 하더라고 꼭 전해다오. 공항에서 처음 회장님 내외분을 뵙을 때 도란이 얘기를 먼저 하시더군. 그리고 곧장 한국식당으로 달려가 점심을 같이 먹고, 호텔에서는 밤늦게까지 얘기 나누며 정말이지 아주 유쾌한 시간을 나누었단다.

아무쪼록 건강히 잘 있고 주위사람들에게 나와 아줌마를 대신해 안부 전해다오. 다음에 다시 만날 날을 기대하며 이만 줄일까 한다.

안녕!

Dear Honorable Rotary Club President,

I'd like to express my gratitude to all Rotarians. I do not know how to thank you for your support, comfort, and hospital visits you have shown while my daughter, Doran, has been recovering from an automobile accident. You have greatly helped us deal with this very difficult situation.

I am not only impressed by your willingness to help my daughter come to the U.S. as the recipient of the Cultural Ambassadorial Scholarship, but I am also deeply impressed by the sacred spirit and activities of the Rotary Club. When I return to South Korea, I will become a member of Ilsan Rotary Club in Gungi-Do and will try repay to our community, the warm service, and love you have shown.

Once again I wish your club prosperity, and am deeply thankful for your love and support. God bless you and thank you so much!

Sincerely,

Hwan-Gu Lee, father of Doran Lee

존경하는 로터리클럽 회장님,

그리고 회원 여러분께 감사의 인사를 드립니다. 금번 저의 큰딸 도란이의 교통사고 치료와 수습과정에서 여러분께서 보여주신 문병방문과 위로와 지원에 대하여 무엇으로 감사해야 할지 모르겠습니다.

저의 딸이 E.L.S.장학생으로 오도록 도와주시고, 사고에 물심양면으로 힘써주심을 통하여 로터리클럽의 숭고한 정신과 활동에 감동하였습니다.

제가 한국으로 돌아가면, 제가 살고 있는 경기도 일산지역의 로터리클럽에 가입하고 활동함으로써, 여러분으로부터 받은 따뜻한 봉사와 사랑을 어려운 이웃께 돌려드리도록 노력하겠습니다.

다시 한번 여러분의 로터리클럽이 더욱 발전하기를 기원 드리며, 여러분의 사랑의 지원과 성원에 깊은 감사의 인사를 드립니다.

하나님의 사랑과 은혜가 항상 함께 하시기를 기원합니다. 감사합니다.

도란아빠 이환구 올림

2007, 12, 7

Dear R.I. President D.K. Lee

안녕하세요 회장님, 저는 로터리 3750 지구의 문화사절장학생 이도란이라고 합니다. 먼저 회장님께서 로터리인터내셔널의 첫 번째 총재가 되신 것을 축하 드립니다.

제가 이렇게 회장님께 글을 올리는 이유는 제가 로터리와 맺게 된 소중한 인연과 로터리가 저에게 준 소중한 기회들에 감사하기 위해서랍니다.

저는 현재 이화여대 영문과 3학년에 재학중인 데, 작년 7월 로터리장학생으로 6개월간 미국에서 생활하게 되었습니다. 부족한 것이 많은 저에게 로터리는 제 인생에 있어 참으로 귀중한 경험을 주었고, 좋은 분들을 많이 만나게 해 주었습니다.

6개월간 전 테네시주에 있는 내쉬빌이라는 곳에서 어학연수과정을 거치며 미국의 생활을 체험하고, 여러 로터리클럽들을 방문하여 한국과, 제 경험을 알렸습니다. 때마침 이번에 회장님께서 이번 주에 내쉬빌을 방문하신다는 이야기를 듣고 많이 반가웠답니다. 또 제가 미국에 있을 때, 저의 호스트 로터리안 (Host Rotarian)이셨던 김기현선생님 (Hendersonville 로터리클럽)께서 며칠간 회장님의 수행을 맡게 되셨다는 이야기를 들었어요. 미국에서는 한국인 로터리안을 만나기 어렵다고 들었는데, 마침 또 그리 크지 않은 내쉬빌에 만난 김기현 선생님은 저에게 가족 같은 은인이시거든요.

내쉬빌은 작지만 참 정감 있는 도시이고, 친절하고 좋은 사람들이 많은 도시였어요. 하지만 낯선 땅에 유학생의 신분으로 혼자 6개월을 지낸다는 것이 처음에는 많이 낯설고 두려웠어요. 그때 만난 제 호스트 로터리안 김선생님, 그리고 그

가족들께서는 절 친 가족보다 더 따뜻하게 맞아주시고 돌봐주셨답니다.

무엇보다 제가 그분들과, 그곳의 모든 로터리클럽에 감사하는 것은, 지난 11월 Thanksgiving 날 밤에 제가 큰 교통사고를 당했을 때 많은 도움을 주셨기 때문입니다. 친구의 미숙한 운전으로 뒷자석에서 잠이 들었던 저는 고속도로에서 큰 사고를 당했고, 그 때문에 그곳에 있는 벤더필트병원 (Vanderbilt)에서 몇 번의 큰 수술을 받고 생사의 기로에 섰었습니다. 한국에 있는 부모님께서 며칠 뒤에 미국에 도착했지만 의식도 없고, 가족도 없는 저를 김선생님과 많은 로터리안들이 돌보아주셨어요. 처음에 심각한 상태에 놓였을 때 누구보다 김선생님께서는, 단지 저의 호스트 로터리안이라는 이유에도 불구하고, 먼저 달려와 모든 일을 해결하기 위해 애쓰셨어요. 퇴원 후에도 제가 있던 홈스테이 (Home Stay) 가정에서 나와 김선생님 댁에서 제 어머니와 함께 머물렀는데 김선생님 가족들은 너무 편하게, 따뜻하게 대해 주셨습니다.

또한 Hendersonville Rotary Club을 중심으로 한 많은 로터리 클럽과 회원들이, 저를 위해 기도하고, 병원을 방문할 뿐 아니라 어마어마한 병원비를 위해 모금을 하고 진심 어린 위로를 해주셨습니다. 비록 사고는 제 인생에 있어 큰 시련이고 고비였지만, 로터리가 만들어 준 인연들을 통해 전 무엇보다 소중한 것들을 많이 깨달았고 큰 사랑을 받았어요. 덕분에 지금은 많이 회복이 되어 한국에 무사히 돌아왔답니다.

로터리는 저에게 큰 기회이자, 인연이자, 사랑입니다. 그래서 또한, 이런 국제로터리의 한국인 총재님이 되신 이동건 회장님께도 진심으로 감사 드리고, 축하 드립니다. 회장님께서도, 제겐 너무나도 소중한 곳인 내쉬빌에서, 의미 있고 좋은 시간을 보내시길 진심으로 바랍니다. 그럼 이만 글을 줄이겠습니다. 안녕히 계세요.

2007 문화사절 장학생 이도란 올림

Dear Rotarians

Hello Rotarians. This is Doran Lee from Korea, the Rotary Cultural Ambassadorial Scholar of six months. Time passed like an arrow, and it has already been about 6 months since I first came to Nashville. Thanks to all Rotarians, I have precious memories and experiences from this beautiful city. I not only learned English and the American culture but I also met wonderful people.

However, I had an automobile accident last thanksgiving, and I had to have surgery on my brain and face. Fortunately, my recovery has been very fast, and I am very happy about that. Though it has been a hard time for me and my parents, I have also learned many things from real experience. I realized the love and care from all the people around me. My host Rotarian and his family always treated me and my family as real family. Also, many Rotarians visited the hospital I was staying in and showed their concerns. Rotary helped me so much both physically and spiritually.

I do not know how to express my thanks to all Rotarians. The only thing I can do now is to become healthy. After I get healthy, I want to devote myself to help others in the future like Rotarians.

Thank you again, and happy New Year.

Doran Lee

Letter to Korean Rotarians

한국인회원에게,

　얼굴 한번 본적 없는 한국인회원에게, 그것도 미국 내에서 한글로 쓴 나의 글을 읽을 기회가 거의 없을 것이라는 것을 알면서 굳이 속마음을 글로 드러내놓는 것은 나 자신의 마음 속 거울을 깨끗하게 간직하고 픈 소망 때문입니다. 열일곱 살에 미국으로 이민오기 전까지 로터리회원들이 살고 있는 지역사회와 세계에 공허한 업적을 남기고 있는 것을 신문지상으로 익히 들어 알고 있습니다만 정작 로터리회원을 만난 적은 한번도 없었습니다. 제가 고등학교 3 학년때 한국을 떠났으니 아마도 사회생활이 없어서 일 것입니다.

　뜻 깊고 알차게 보낸 2008 년 6 월, 곧 이면 가고 새로운 로터리 2008-2009 년이 시작됩니다. 로터리외원으로써 걸어온 나의 발자취를 뒤돌아 보고 정리하다 보니 늘 그랬듯이 자부심보다 후회 감이, 떳떳함보다 아쉬움이 더 큰 자국으로 남아 있군요. 로터리클럽에 처음으로 참여하면서 자신의 부족함 때문에 많은 것을 도울 수 없었지만 로터리 정신 하나로 뭉친 회원들의 자아봉사정신에 많은 것을 배우고 깨우치게 되었습니다.

　한국인회원 여러분,

　만추국이라는 꽃을 보신적이 있으신지요? 이 꽃은 다른 꽃들이 저마다 앞다퉈 피고 질 때 꽃봉오리를 꼭 다물고 있다가 아주 늦은 매서운 겨울이 되어서야 활짝 피는 꽃이랍니다. 꽃마다 저마다의 아름다움과 추함을 가지고 있는 법인데

만추국은 보는 사람의 마음에 꼭 드는 색깔과 향기, 그리고 아름다움으로 핀 다는군요. 한때의 실패와 좌절감 때문에 노력조차 포기하고 주저앉아버린 그런 사람들은 볼 수 없는 꽃입니다. Robert Frost 라는 시인은 삶을 세 단어로 결론 지었습니다. "I can sum up everything I have learned about life. It goes on." 어떠한 어려움에 처하든 자신과 남의 삶에 등을 도려서는 안됩니다. 삶은 난을 치듯 하나하나 일구어나가야 하는 것이니까요.

회원 여러분, 어떻게 보면 우리가 하는 일이 전혀 가치 없이 느껴질 때가 있습니다. 우리가 계획하고 세운 목적이 그르다면 실패는 당연한 일이겠으나, 우리가 세운 목적이 옳다면 그때는 알 수 없어도 언젠가는 반드시 이루게 될 것입니다. 그렇기 때문에 우리는 우리가 세운 목적에 비관이나 낙망을 해서는 안됩니다. 목적의 달성을 염원하면서 실패할 것을 우려하고 생각한다면 우리가 생각하는 그대로 되지 않겠습니까? 우리 세대에 이루어지지 않는다면 다음 세대에 이루어질 것이기 때문이죠. 우리 때에 볼 수 없는 만추국이 다음 세대에 활짝 피어준다면 먼저가는 우리는 하나님께서 우리에게 주신 사명을 다했다고 봅니다.

옛말에 세세생생 이라는 말이 있습니다. 처음에 뜻한 바를 성취하기 위해 몇 번이던지 다시 태어나 노력하고 노력한다는 말입니다. 이 생애에 이루지 못하면 그 다음 생애에 다음 세대사람들이 이루어놓지 않겠습니까? 그래서 큰 나는 죽어도 작은 나는 영원토록 살아남게 되나 봅니다. 우리의 뜻이 옳다면, 우리의 사랑이 진실하다면, 어느 땐가 꼭 거두게 될 것입니다. 열매가 되려고 하지 말고 거름이 되고자 하는 우리는 앞으로도 남을 위해 열심히 일해야 할 것입니다. 이것이 진정 나 자신의 행복이 될 테니까요.

마지막으로 제가 자원봉사단의 한 일원으로 과테말라 (Guatemala)에 가서 들은 얘기를 해드릴까 합니다. 내쉬빌에서 비행기로 네 시간밖에 걸리지 않는 이 나라는 테네시보다 작은 면적에 문맹률이 50 퍼센트도 되지 않습니다. 그 중 85 퍼센트의 인구가 가난 속에 허덕이며 하루 평균 일당 3 달러로 그날그날 살아가고 있습니다. 지상에서 가장 풍부하고 부유한 나라, 미국에서 온 우리 로터리회원들은 오직 가르치고 주러 왔지 그들에게 받을 것이라고는 아무것도 없다고 생각했습니다. 그러나 작년에 이곳에 왔던 로터리회원들이 다시 찾아온 이유는 물질적으로 가난한 그들에게서 풍족하고 부유한 마음을 배웠기 때문입니다. 마음이 가난한 우리에게 부유함과 감사함과 이웃간의 사랑을 느끼게 해준 것은 가난하게 살지언정 서로 도우며 이웃을 위해 사는 그들의 삶이었습니다. 열다섯살인 내 딸과 같이 간 미션여행(Mission Trip), 앞으로도 계속될 것입니다.

한 노인이 자기가 어렸을 때 있었던 일을 들려주었는데…… 자기가 사는 마을에 어느 여자 전도사가 왔답니다. 이 전도사는 한 나무를 가리키면서 자기가 여러 나라를 가보았는데 저렇게 아름다운 나무는 여태껏 본적이 없다고 했습니다. 그러니 자기 앞마당에 심어놓고 두고두고 보고 싶다고 했답니다. 지금 노인이 다 된 이 어린 청년은 그때 비웃으며 말하기를, "전도사님, 저 나무는 성장해 꽃을 피우기까지 백 년이란 세월이 걸린답니다. 그러니 지금 심어보았자 무슨 소용이 있겠습니까?" 잠시 뭔가를 생각한 듯싶던 전도사 하는 말이, "그렇다면 내일까지 기다릴 수가 없겠군요. 지금 당장 심어주세요!" 하더 랍니다. 이 어린 콰테말라청년은 그 후 미국에서 공부를 마친 후 미국에서의 좋은 직장과 안락한 삶을 포기하고 자기나라로 돌아와 전인교육에 전 생애를 바치고 있습니다. 이 나무는 콰테말라 뿐만이 아니라 한국, 미국, 온 세계에도 있을 것입니다. 마음으로 보고 마음으로 피고지는 꽃일 테니까요!

우리 한인이 모두 이런 생각을 가지고 자신과 남을 위해 살아준다면 우리의 마음 속 만추국은 꼭 필 것입니다. 못난 이 글을 읽어주신 것에 감사 드리며 부디 뜻하신 모든 일들이 성사되길 기원하겠습니다. 안녕히 계십시오.

미국에서 김기현 로터리회원

Acknowledgement

My daughter was my first proofreader and editor for this book ever since she was in high school. Also, I asked my two sons, Hannie and Doun to do the same whenever they had time. More than anything else, I enjoyed having long conversations with my children about my life, and that was worth far more than finding errors in my book.

I would like to express my deep gratitude to Headmaster William Slater, language arts teacher Miss. Amber Hunt, and class of 2014 Hendersonville Christian Academy. After reading my rough draft, Mr. Slater and Miss Hunt thought that my book would be a valuable lesson to young minds and a good life experience for them.

This book is proofread and edited by following students at Hendersonville Christian Academy: Elizabeth Hochstetler, Jacob Cole, Tara Erickson, Miguel Rodriguez, Tori Roberts, Eddie Hudson, Zandalee Sayne, Anna Barreiro, Haley Hall, Natalie Baggett, Evan Turtle, Matt Holloway, Holly Johnson, Sara Lei Ding, Emily Davis, Samantha Patton, Elliot Couch, Alec Turc, Zach Mann, Kelsey Raymond, Stephen Hengeli, Juan DaSilva, Briley Berman, Tyler Putty, Felicia Jones, Julia Harmon, Stuart Farless, Christian Norris, Savannah Lindsey, Samuel Miller, Jacob Courtright, Austin Ellis, Zachary Lockwood, Matthew Stidham. I have truly enjoyed open and frank conversations with students in the classroom. I can't wait to see their bright future, and they always will be a part of my life.

This book could not have been completed without the support and encouragement of my fellow Rotarians in District 6760, especially members from my club. Thank you for allowing me to include your heartfelt letters in this book: David Black, Kara Arnold, Brenda Payne, Eddie Roberson, Gayla Zoz, S.T. Womeldorf, Kaye Palmer, Rod Lilly, Jim Campbell, Grace Guthrie, Don Claussen, Harold Peeples, Nick Peeples, Dale Flowers, Keith C. Dennen, Robin William, Joe Beaver, Kent Cochran, Pat Lebkuecher, Tim Lynch, PDG Rufus Clifford M.D.

All 327 incoming district governors and their spouses from over 200 countries attended Rotary International Assembly in San Diego from January 12 to 18, 2014 for the governorship training. I wanted to meet and exchange gifts to as many classmates as possible. Meeting District GovenorJong-Boo Jin and his wife Sun-hui Choi from Korea was one of my highlights. They truly have enriched my life ever since I have known them, and I don't know how I can repay their kindness, humility, and guidance. Most of all, thank you for being my friend.

Last but not least, I would like to thank my dear friend, Dr. James M Perdue, for helping me with self publishing my two books.

About the Author

Kim Kim came to America from Korea at the age of seventeen as a youth exchange student. Despite not knowing any English, he enrolled in a high school in Gallatin, Tennessee and later graduated from Middle Tennessee State University. He has owned and operated several small businesses while he works at the hospital as a director and supervisor.

Since joining Hendersonville Rotary Club in 2000, he has maintained perfect attendance and is a Paul Harris Society Charter Member and Major Donor. His club and district offices includes club president, international service committee chair, youth exchange officer, ambassadorial scholar counselor, the Rotary Foundation Alumni Chair, and District 6760 assistant governor for three years. In July 2014, he became fourth Korean-American District Governor in North America and the first in Tennessee, USA.

Kim is recognized for his remarkable humanitarian efforts to assist those affected by natural disasters as part of the ShelterBox Response Team (SRT) member. In addition, he has traveled to five continents to execute Rotary projects including NID (National Immunization Day) in Africa, the dental/vision/medical mission in Guatemala, and the electricity project in Honduras.

For his outstanding humanitarian efforts, he received Rotarian of the Year, District 6760 Rotarian of the Year, Lifetime Distinguished Service Award, the Frist Humanitarian Award, the Tennessee Hospital Association Meritorious Service Award, the President's Volunteer Service Award from President Barack Obama, and Rotary's highest honor the Service Above Self Award.

Kim is active in his community. He is a CASA (Court Appointed Special Advocates) volunteer, on the United Way Allocation board, the Executive director of Korean-American Social Services, and a member of the Leadership Sumner board of directors.

Kim briefly returned to Korea in 1988 to marry his wife Sue in an arranged marriage, and they have one daughter and two sons.